THE COMPLETE GUIDE TO
ALASKAN MALAMUTES

Coreen Martineau and
Jordan Honeycutt

LP Media Inc. Publishing

Text copyright © 2020 by LP Media Inc.

www.lpmedia.org

Publication Data

Coreen Martineau And Jordan Honeycutt

The Complete Guide to Alaskan Malamutes ---- First edition.

Summary: "Successfully raising a Alaskan Malamute dog from puppy to old age" --- Provided by publisher.

ISBN: 978-1-952069-08-6

[1. Alaskan Malamutes --- Non-Fiction] I. Title.

This book has been written with the published intent to provide accurate and author-itative information in regard to the subject matter included. While every reasonable pre-caution has been taken in preparation of this book the author and publisher expressly dis-claim responsibility for any errors, omissions, or adverse effects arising from the use or application of the information contained inside. The techniques and suggestions are to be used at the reader's discretion and are not to be considered a substitute for professional veterinary care. If you suspect a medical problem with your dog, consult your veterinarian.

Design by Sorin Rădulescu

First paperback edition, 2020

Cover Photo Courtesy of Marie Jontz - Estekwalan Alaskan Malamutes

TABLE OF CONTENTS

CHAPTER 1
History of the Alaskan Malamute 8
Physical Characteristics 13
Behavioral Characteristics 14
Is a Malamute the Right Breed for You? 14

CHAPTER 2
Choosing an Alaskan Malamute 18
Cost of Ownership 18
Buying vs. Adopting 21
   Adoption 21
   Choosing a Breeder 27
The Different Puppy Personality Types 33
Tests for Evaluating Your Malamute Puppy 36

CHAPTER 3
Preparing for Your New Malamute 40
Pre-Puppy Preparation 40
Rules and Routines 41
Preparing Your Home 43
Puppy-Proofing Your Home 43
Dangerous Things Your Dog Might Eat 47
Preparing an Outdoor Space 49
Preparing Children and Other Pets 49
Supplies to Purchase Before You Bring Your Malamute Home 51

CHAPTER 4

Bringing Your Malamute Home 54

Picking Up Your Malamute 55

The Ride Home 55

Your Malamute's First Night 57

Choosing the Right Veterinarian 59

The First Vet Visit 61

CHAPTER 5

Being a Puppy Parent 62

Have Realistic Expectations 63

Chewing 65

Digging 65

Running Away 67

Howling, Barking, and Growling 68

Separation Anxiety 69

Crate Training Basics 70

CHAPTER 6

Alaskan Malamutes and Your Other Pets 74

Introducing Your Malamute to Other Animals 74

Introducing an Older Dog 76

The Pack Mentality 77

Bad Behavior – How to Correct It 79

Rough Play or Aggression? 80

How to Break Up a Dog Fight 81

    Use Loud Noises 81

    Spray Them with Water 81

    Wheelbarrow Method 81

What Happens if My Pets Don't Get Along? 82

CHAPTER 7

Socializing Your New Malamute 84

Importance of Socialization 84

Behavior Around Other Dogs 85

Safe Ways to Socialize 87

Socializing Adult Dogs **89**

Dog Parks **90**

Meeting New People **91**

Alaskan Malamutes and Children **93**

CHAPTER 8

Physical and Mental Exercise **94**

Exercise Requirements **94**

How to Make Exercise Fun **95**

Importance of Mental Exercise **97**

Tips for Keeping Your Malamute Occupied **97**

Dog Sports and Activities **100**

    Sledding or Mushing **100**

    Skijoring **102**

    Hiking and Backpacking **102**

CHAPTER 9

Training Your Alaskan Malamute **104**

Consistency and Routine **104**

Benefits of Proper Training **105**

Training Methods **106**

    Alpha Dog Training **106**

    Positive Reinforcement **107**

Which Method is Best for Your Malamute **108**

    Primary Reinforcement **109**

    Secondary Reinforcement **109**

    Dangers of Correcting Using Punishment **109**

Basic Commands **111**

    Sit **111**

    Down **111**

    Heel **113**

    Stay **113**

    Leave It **113**

When and How to Hire a Trainer **114**

    Owner Expectations **114**

    Obedience Classes **114**

CHAPTER 10
Dealing with Unwanted Behaviors **116**
What Is Considered Bad Behavior in Dogs? **116**
Finding the Root of the Problem **119**
How to Properly Correct Your Dog **121**
When to Call a Professional **121**

CHAPTER 11
Traveling with Your Alaskan Malamute **122**
Flying with Your Malamute **122**
Hotel Stays with Your Malamute **124**
Kenneling vs. Dog Sitters **125**
Choosing the Right Boarding Facility **126**
Special Tips and Tricks for Traveling **127**

CHAPTER 12
Nutrition **130**
Importance of Good Diet **130**
The Pros and Cons of Commercial Dog Food **132**
    Ingredients to Avoid **133**
Homemade Dog Food **135**
Giving Your Dog Human Food **137**
Weight Management **138**

CHAPTER 13
Basic Healthcare and Grooming **140**
Visiting the Vet **140**
Vaccinations **141**
Fleas and Ticks **142**
Coat Basics **144**
Bathing and Brushing **145**
Dental Care **147**
Nail Trimming **147**
Cleaning the Ears and Eyes **148**
Common Diseases and Health Conditions **149**
Holistic Alternatives and Supplements **149**

Herbs **150**
Pet Insurance. **151**

CHAPTER 14

Caring for Your Senior Dog **152**
Common Old-Age Ailments **153**
Basic Senior Dog Care **154**
Illness and Injury Prevention **155**
Supplements and Nutrition **157**
When It's Time to Say Goodbye **159**
How will you know when the time is right? **159**
The Euthanasia Process **160**

CHAPTER 1
History of the Alaskan Malamute

The Alaskan Malamute is a member of the Spitz group. The origin of the Spitz group is largely unknown, but it is believed these dogs originated in the Arctic and Siberia. Originally bred to work with humans, Malamutes assisted by hunting bears, seals, and walrus as well as pulling sleds. These broad-shouldered, muscular dogs are one of the oldest working sled dog breeds in the Arctic and can pull anywhere from 1,100 to 3,300 lbs, depending on the size and training of the dog. According to the American Kennel Club (AKC), Malamutes are believed to be descended from the domesticated wolf-dogs that migrated with the Paleolithic hunters from Siberia into North America an estimated 4,000 years ago.

The Mahlemut tribe, a nomadic Inuit tribe in the Kotzebue Sound in northwestern Alaska, is credited today with cultivating and raising this breed. This is the tribe from which the Malamute got its name. These people formed close relationships with their dogs and relied heavily on them for survival in the tough Alaskan weather conditions. The Mahlemut peo-

Photo Courtesy of Magdalena Lewandowska, Photo by Israel Patino

Photo Courtesy of
Doris Thompson

ple are said to have kept these dogs guarded and did not allow them to cross breed with dogs of other tribes. Legend even says the Mahlemut people may have occasionally left their dogs in the wild at night in hopes they would breed with the wolf to create a stronger dog.

Whether the legend is true or not may never be known, but scientists today believe the Malamute to be a purebred domestic dog and not part wolf. However, since the Malamute was not bred for a specific purpose like many other breeds, the breed was allowed to keep the traits that helped it survive and thrive in harsh Alaskan winters. This may make the dogs more similar in nature to their wild wolf ancestors after all.

Because the Mahlemut people and their dogs depended on each other so heavily, Malamutes became a part of the tribe themselves, often treated like the humans. Although food was scarce and they were often hungry, the dogs always got their share of the kill. This close dependency and trust in each other contributed to the generally friendly, people-loving temperament of the Malamute today, a trait that is not common in other Spitz type dogs.

When the Klondike gold rush started in the 1900s, the demand for dogs that could pull heavy freight loads increased exponentially. Because the Mahlemut tribe kept their dogs so guarded and put such a high price on them, their numbers were small and the demand could not quickly be filled. This led to prospectors crossbreeding the Malamutes with other dogs to cre-

Photo Courtesy of
Adam Monument

ate their sled teams. This is what many people believe was the demise of the Inuit village dog.

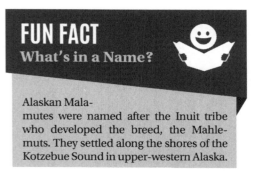

FUN FACT

What's in a Name?

Alaskan Malamutes were named after the Inuit tribe who developed the breed, the Mahlemuts. They settled along the shores of the Kotzebue Sound in upper-western Alaska.

Along with the gold rush came a new interest in sled racing and weight pulling competitions. The dogs the Mahlemut people had once relied so heavily on for survival were being crossbred with dogs from all over the world in an effort to make them faster and stronger for competition. This crossbreeding almost wiped out the dog we now know as the Alaskan Malamute.

There are two main lines from which today's Alaskan Malamute originates; the Kotzebue line and the M'Loot line. Kotzebue Malamutes originated from the Mahlemut peoples' dogs in the Kotzebue region in northeastern Alaska. This is thought to be the original line of Malamutes that was sold and eventually almost destroyed by the Klondike gold rush prospectors. Eva "Short" Seeley fell in love with the dogs and took over the breeding from Arthur Walden through the Chinook Kennels. Seeley, a school teacher in Massachusetts in 1923, was instrumental in reviving the breed. Eventually, alongside her husband, Milton, she became the most famous breeder of Alaskan Malamutes in the United States. Her work to revive the breed led to the AKC's recognition of the breed in 1935. Only the Malamutes of the Kotzebue line were recognized at this point.

A breeder named Paul Voelker established another line of malamutes called the M'Loot line. M'Loot Malamutes were a bit different both in appearance and temperament. M'Loots were taller and narrower with bigger ears and longer noses. While the Kotzebue line showed only grey, wolf-like coats, the M'Loot line came in a variety of colors. M'Loots also tended to be a bit more aggressive than the Kotzebue. Voelker did not pursue AKC recognition so the Kotzebue remained the only recognized line of Malamutes at this time.

A third line appeared when Robert Zoller decided to cross the Kotzebue and the M'Loot, in an attempt to take the best traits from each. This line, known as the Hinman line, also birthed some of the foundation dogs for the breed we now know as the Alaskan Malamute.

During World War II, Malamutes joined the war effort. Many dogs were loaned for expeditions to support the country. After the dogs had served their purpose, the American government ordered the dogs to be tied to an ice floe and destroyed. This tragic decision nearly incited a riot among many of the U.S. Navy men who had worked with the animals. After recognizing that the breed was nearly wiped out again by this action, the AKC opened registration to Malamutes of all lines in an attempt to revive the breed once again.

For a period of time after the tragic destruction of the dogs, the AKC recognized dogs of all lines as long as they could prove their quality by attaining ten championship points. Many dogs were registered during this time, but soon after the AKC once again closed registration to all lines except the Kotzebue. All Malamutes today originate from Kotzebue Malamutes or the Malamutes registered during this open period.

Many people today believe that it is nearly impossible to find a Malamute that is pure in origin from one singular line. Most are believed to be a combination of all three lines. In 2010 Alaska officially recognized the Malamute as the state dog.

Photo Courtesy of
Barry Wanless

Photo Courtesy of
Chelsea Murray

Physical Characteristics

Alaskan Malamutes are powerfully built dogs. They have a proud stance with an upright head, alert eyes that shine with intelligence and curiosity, a broad head, triangular upright ears, and a bulky muzzle. Their coat is thick, with a coarse outercoat and a wooly undercoat that keeps them warm even in the coldest temperatures. They have very distinct facial features, often with a "mask" or "bar" above their eyebrows. The tail is very furry, carried up over the back and resembles what has been called a "waving plume." They are heavy boned dogs with sound legs, large feet, a deep, powerful chest, and large shoulders. Their gait is steady, balanced, and appears to be completely efficient and tireless.

Male Malamutes usually stand between 24-26 inches tall and weigh around 80-85 pounds. Females are slightly smaller, standing between 22-24 inches tall, weighing between 70-75 pounds. They come in a variety of coat colors, ranging from light gray to black, as well as sable and shades of red. White is the predominant color on the underbody, legs, feet, tail, and facial markings.

Behavioral Characteristics

"Alaskan Malamutes are a conundrum of opposites. They can be couch potatoes that will sleep all day, but destructive monsters if you don't exercise and stimulate their minds. They are very vocal dogs that will talk and sing to you all day, but make terrible watch dogs. They are very intelligent and learn fast, but then pick and choose when they want to listen. They will frustrate you to no end, and yet you will fall in love with them more and more."

Brian Trujillo
Trujillo's Malamutes

Alaskan Malamutes are known for their wonderful and friendly temperaments, as well as their stubbornness and independence. They have been called teddy bear dogs for their love of snuggling and affection, especially from children. They have no natural aggression towards humans and because of this they tend to make extremely poor guard dogs. Many people can be intimidated by their sheer size; however, they are more likely to invite a stranger in and show him the silver than try to scare him away.

Is a Malamute the Right Breed for You?

"They are thinkers and problem solvers. They enjoy digging and playing in the water. They love to hike and be in the outdoors. They are strong and kind. They are stubborn and retain something that is still wild at heart. They bond with their owner to form a lifelong companion and partnership. They are hard workers and love to be included in everything their family does."

Gail Partain
Windwalker Malamutes

Malamutes are highly independent and intelligent dogs who like to think for themselves, and they are not naturally obedient. A Malamute owner must work hard to earn a dog's trust and respect. You must establish your "alpha dog" status early and work to maintain it throughout your dog's life.

Malamutes will naturally seek to follow a strong leader who is calm and reliable that they know they can trust and respect. However, if they cannot find a leader they consider worthy of following, Malamutes will lead themselves.

Bred to work a very important job, Malamutes have a very high exercise need. Without substantial mental and physical stimulation, Malamutes have a tendency to become bored and destructive. You may find that boredom manifests itself in ripped up couch cushions or a backyard full of craters.

While Malamutes may act friendly toward every person they encounter, they do not tend to have the same level of affection for other dogs. As pack animals, Malamutes thrive on pack order and like to be the alphas of the house. Malamutes can become very aggressive with other dogs, especially those of the same sex. While Malamutes can live harmoniously with other dogs if they are introduced at a young age, it is not advisable to introduce a mature Malamute to a home with existing pets.

Another common trait among this breed is a strong predatory drive. If allowed to run loose, they could become a neighborhood menace. In rural areas, they can harass, attack, or kill livestock and wildlife. In urban areas, they can become a deadly threat to neighborhood cats and other small animals.

They can also be surprisingly clever escape artists and need to be kept behind a tall, secure fence. Malamutes can scale a 6-8 foot tall wall with minimal effort. If your Malamute manages to escape, he is not likely to return of his own incentive for quite a while due to his independent and curious nature.

Malamutes can be difficult to live with and challenging to train. They are strong-willed and stubborn, requiring a strong leader who can take charge and enforce the rules. Malamutes tend to challenge the established hierarchy if the owner has not established himself as the pack leader. Malamutes need an owner who will stand up to challenges and

Photo Courtesy of Elizabeth Hendrix
Photo by Barbara O'Brien Photography

Photo Courtesy of
Eryn Morgan

demand respect and obedience. If he sees an opportunity to manipulate or control a situation, and you have not established yourself as alpha, he will attempt to take the dominant position.

Some families find Malamutes to be "too much dog" for them to manage and end up surrendering the dog to a shelter. Malamutes start out as small, soft and cuddly, but they quickly grow into powerful, independent-thinking adult dogs. Be sure you are ready for the responsibility of an Alaskan Malamute before you adopt or buy to avoid the unnecessary heartbreak of surrendering a family pet.

Malamutes are not suitable for living in an apartment. They are incredibly active and need a lot of exercise to thrive in a home environment. They are happiest when they have a job to do. This could be pulling a sled, hauling a pack, or simply walking by your side. If they do not get enough daily activity, along with a good amount of mental stimulation, they will quickly become bored and restless.

Malamutes also have a passion for digging and will make themselves a "nest" or a "den" in your yard if left to their own devices. Alaskan Malamutes are not a breed that will be satisfied with a short walk around the block and a few ball throws. They also tend to howl if left alone for too long. Malamutes are exuberant talkers and can make a variety of different sounds, usually at a high volume.

Because of their thick, wooly double layer coats, Malamutes require several hours of dedicated grooming every week. While they can survive in warmer climates, they were bred to survive and thrive in extremely cold

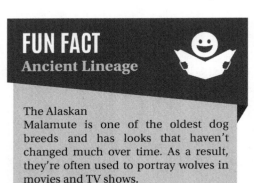

FUN FACT
Ancient Lineage

The Alaskan Malamute is one of the oldest dog breeds and has looks that haven't changed much over time. As a result, they're often used to portray wolves in movies and TV shows.

temperatures. They are very heavy shedders and will shed their entire undercoat all at once, twice a year. Grooming during this time can be time consuming and messy.

Alaskan Malamutes can make wonderful family pets and are often wonderful and patient with children. Just as with any other breed, Malamutes come with their share of joys and challenges. If you've considered the above characteristics and believe you can provide the care and authority your Malamute will need, you will be rewarded with a wonderfully affectionate, loyal and hard-working dog.

Photo Courtesy of Ana Maria Ciulcu

CHAPTER 2
Choosing an Alaskan Malamute

Cost of Ownership

Many dog owners completely underestimate how expensive it is to own and properly care for an Alaskan Malamute. Most of the time the only thing that is taken into consideration is the initial purchase price. While this is definitely a factor, there are a number of other expenses that need to be considered as well. Your Malamute is completely dependent on you for everything, and it's important to be prepared for all of the responsibilities and financial requirements that come with having a Malamute in your life.

Besides the initial purchase price for your puppy, or the adoption fee to the shelter, there are also the basic supplies that a Malamute puppy needs. Food costs will vary depending on what brand you choose to buy, but cost on average $400-$700 for a dog the size of a Malamute. Keep in mind other costs such as toys, chewable bones, collar, tags, leash, food, water bowls, and more.

Vet bills are typically the biggest expense for dog owners. Depending on where you live, the office fee is about $50 and an exam can be upwards of $100. A spay or neuter operation can cost up to $200. Vaccines are relatively cheap at $20-$30 each, but testing for anything from heartworm to diagnostic blood work can cost anywhere from $20-$250. If there is a more serious illness or injury, things can get incredibly expensive in a hurry. X-rays and ultrasounds can cost up to $300-$400. Anesthesia and surgery procedures for emergency situations can run into the thousands of dollars. Pet insurance can help offset some of these costs but can cost an average of $500-$600 per year.

Also consider the cost of boarding your Malamute when you are away for an extended period of time. If you travel often and do not plan to take your dog, these costs can add up quickly. Look into local boarding facilities to find pricing for your area.

There can also be costs associated with living with your dog. Leasing agents and landlords usually require a pet deposit when you sign your lease, and these usually run $200-$700.

Grooming is another expense that needs to be considered. A bath is relatively inexpensive at $20-$40, but anything more than that can be quite costly. A brush and trim can be as much as $120, and it can be much higher when a Malamute is blowing his undercoat each year.

Training can also be an unexpected cost. Whether you decide to train your Malamute yourself or opt to seek assistance from a professional (which is definitely highly recommended for all first time Malamute owners) an hour with a private in-home trainer will cost around $100 per session, while a 6-week long group class costs an average of $200-$300.

While many of the above costs are optional, it is still wise to consider all of the potential costs of owning and raising your Malamute before you bring him home. You may also be able to save some money by preparing ahead of time. Instead of buying a brand new crate, check online garage sale sites to see if anyone has one for sale. If you have considered the cost of ownership and believe you can care for your Malamute properly, the next step is finding your dog!

Photo Courtesy of
Denise Martin

Buying vs. Adopting

The question of whether it is better to buy a dog or adopt one is an incredibly old debate, one with loyal and adamant supporters on both sides, and it can cause intense feelings in everyone involved. Some say that it is a moral and ethical issue, while others say that it is merely a matter of preference and practicality.

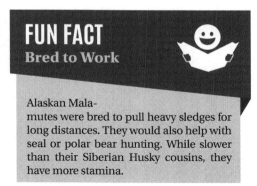

FUN FACT
Bred to Work

Alaskan Malamutes were bred to pull heavy sledges for long distances. They would also help with seal or polar bear hunting. While slower than their Siberian Husky cousins, they have more stamina.

Adoption

Adopting a Malamute puppy from a shelter or rescue can be a highly rewarding experience. Adopting a dog allows you the joy of saving not one life, but two. Not only do you save the life of the dog that you have adopted, but you also save the life of the dog who gets to take its place in the shelter.

There are some disadvantages to adoption, however, if you do manage to find a Malamute from the shelter. The origins, pedigree, and background of most rescue dogs are a mystery. You won't know if your new dog is a purebred or a mixture of several different breeds. If you have found a puppy, you have no way of knowing how big he or she is going to get, or what type of temperament may emerge over time. There is also no way of knowing what has happened to the pup in the past and whether it may have experienced damaging or traumatizing events before coming into your life. Bad experiences can potentially lead to profoundly serious personality or behavioral problems, and something that happened several years ago may still have the potential to trigger your dog, causing social issues or aggression.

Malamutes that have been damaged or traumatized often reflect their pain in a variety of ways. With careful management and consistent training, combined with a lot of patience and love, these poor dogs can be rehabilitated and find their rightful place in the world and in your home. The effort and time that these dogs require is no match for the devotion and companionship they give you in return for your efforts.

Adult Malamutes from an animal shelter have the advantage of age and possibly, training. With an adult Malamute, you can know the temperament and tolerance the dog has for other people and animals. Remem-

Photo Courtesy of
Bronwyn Hinder

ber, Malamutes can be highly aggressive and territorial toward other dogs and small animals, so you will need to take extra care if bringing your mature Malamute into a home with existing pets. You may want to ask the shelter if you can take the dog home for a "test run" to see how he reacts to your existing pets before committing to ownership.

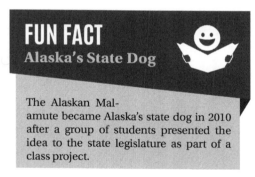

FUN FACT

Alaska's State Dog

The Alaskan Malamute became Alaska's state dog in 2010 after a group of students presented the idea to the state legislature as part of a class project.

Shelter dogs come with all required vaccinations and shots, and are always spayed or neutered before leaving the shelter. Sometimes they are even microchipped.

The Differences Between Animal Shelters and Rescue Organizations

In the United States, there are three different classifications for pet and animal rescues:

Municipal Shelters – These house stray, abandoned animals, and animals surrendered by their owners. They are run and funded by the local government. The animals there have a limited time to be adopted along with an extremely high turnover rate. These shelters usually euthanize animals.

No-Kill Shelter – These are private organizations that will not kill a healthy and adoptable animal. They have a limited intake policy and end up turning many animals away because they just do not have the space to house them. They do not euthanize animals.

Non-Profit Rescue Organizations – These have only a few staff members and are mostly run and operated by volunteers. They try to utilize foster houses as much as they can to save as many animals as possible. They do not euthanize animals.

Municipal Shelters

These are usually government run facilities and a few of them utilize foster homes in their programs. They house their animals on site in a kennel-like environment. Most of them have veterinarians on staff that supply basic medical care as well as spay and neuter operations. They are run and funded by the government with a paid staff who are supplemented by a regiment of volunteers who walk, exercise, and socialize the dogs, as well as clean the facility. They have a set of rules and guidelines for their adoption policies with cheap to moderate adoption fees. Some of them run background checks and a few of them request to meet with the family and any existing pets before adoption to measure compatibility. Almost all of them require an animal be spayed or neutered before it is able to be adopted.

Shelters are a convenient way to find a new pet in your local area as they have a physical facility people can visit and view several animals at one time. The downside to this, however, is that they have limited space and a massive overpopulation problem. The cages and kennels are usually on the small side to make it possible to squeeze in as many animals as possible. The environment is highly stressful with continuous loud barking which can negatively affect a dog's behavior. Dogs can develop what is known as "Kennel Syndrome" and appear fearful or aggressive instead of reflecting their true personality.

Most facilities try to do at least minimal behavior testing to determine how a dog will react to various scenarios, such as a human putting their hand in a food bowl, or a wheelchair going by; any animal that exhibits the least bit of aggression is almost immediately euthanized. Several million dogs and cats are euthanized every year simply because they were not adopted within the 1-2 weeks allotted to them when they came in. There is simply nowhere else for these unwanted animals to go. Pet overpopulation is a severe problem in this country, as there are just too many animals and not enough homes and loving families to adopt them.

No-Kill Shelters

These shelters do not euthanize their animals, and as a result, they often end up turning away many of them. Some no-kill shelters will house animals on site for weeks or even months, sometimes as long as years. Being kept in a high-stress, noisy, and confined environment with minimal amounts of socialization and exercise can have a negative impact on the animals, especially when they are housed in the environment for extended periods of time. They become depressed and withdrawn, or aggressive and reactive, neither of which is appealing to potential adopters.

No-kill shelters try to utilize foster homes as much as possible as a way to get animals out of the kennel environment and into a more home-like environment. Foster owners help train the foster dogs and improve their behavior in an effort to make them more adoptable. Fosterers get to know their animals much better than the average shelter staff or volunteer and can offer invaluable advice and insight during the adoption process. They can be a huge help when trying to find the best, most suitable home for each individual animal.

Non-Profit Rescue Organizations

These organizations are typically privately funded or dependent on donations and support from the community. Some rescues are breed-specific, dedicated to saving one specific breed such as Alaskan Malamutes. Rescues often offer the same medical care and spay and neuter services as municipal shelters do, but only a few of them have an actual veterinarian on staff and most of them have to pay full price for medical care, which gets incredibly expensive. The vast majority of rescue groups rely heavily on foster families to house their dogs and some may not have a physical facility at all, but instead a website with information about their available and adoptable dogs. Because the dogs live with foster families, more is usually known about the dog and their personality, which makes it easier to find a suitable, compatible home for them.

Rescues usually have much higher adoption fees than shelters do because rescues invest much more time and resources into their animals than the average shelter does. They also have much stricter adoption guidelines and policies and ask a variety of questions about the potential adopters. Many of them also have policies in place that require an adopter to return the dog to the rescue if they can no longer keep the animal, rather than selling it or surrendering it to a shelter. A lot of rescues even require a home inspection before they will agree to release an animal to an adopter, and they will send someone out to the potential adopter's home to make sure it is suitable.

Many rescues remain in contact with the adopter for several months and some may return between 3-6 months after the adoption takes place to do another home inspection to make sure that things are going well and that the dog is happy and healthy.

Many homeless animals end up that way through no fault of their own. A family will get a dog only to learn that their landlord does not allow dogs, and they end up needing to get rid of it. Or perhaps their job transferred them to a different state, and they are unable to take the dog with them for assorted reasons. Dogs like these are typically highly adoptable and most have few behavior problems, if any at all.

Choosing whether to adopt your Malamute or purchase from a breeder is a decision that only you and your family can make. Take time to discuss the merits and flaws of each choice. Do your research and get to know your local Malamute breeders, animal shelters, humane societies, and nearby rescue organizations. Breed clubs can be excellent resources for finding a reliable breeder. Talk to friends and family who have experience with dogs, or get advice from your neighborhood vet, groomer, trainer, or pet store. These people have connections in the world of dogs and may be privy to insider information that others do not have about who is recommended and who should be avoided.

It takes time and research to find the perfect Malamute to fit into your family. Do not rush the decision. It is one that will have an enormous impact on your family for years. You do not want to end up with a Malamute that is not compatible with you, your family, or your lifestyle.

Photo Courtesy of
Karen Raines

Tips for Adopting an Alaskan Malamute

If you have your heart set on adopting an Alaskan Malamute, there are a number of resources available to you. First, check with MalamuteRescue. org. They have a list of numerous Malamutes rescue organizations searchable by state. You can also check with any reputable Malamute breeder; they should know if there are any local rescues in your area. Remember that many of the rescue Malamutes will be elderly, disabled, chronically ill, or all of the above. The majority of these dogs have been turned in because their owners can't afford the time or money it takes to care for an ailing, poorly bred dog. While the dogs will present special challenges to care for, they will still provide you with the love you can expect from the Malamute breed.

Choosing a Breeder

"Make sure you talk to a few breeders to get a feel for them, hoping they too will ask you questions. As a breeder I like to know what type of household you have rowdy or calm. Malamutes are not your cookie cutter breed so each Malamute won't fit in every home."

Christy Nash
Oregon Malamutes

If you decide to buy your new Malamute from a breeder, how do you find the right one?

Talk to your vet or other dog professional to see if they can recommend a reputable breeder. They often have experience with breeders and dog owners that can help to point you in the right direction. Dog breed clubs generally have a directory or list of breeders in the area and will be happy to help you with whatever you may need.

Another option is to try to find a breeder online. There are a variety of lists and directories to help get you started. Most professional breeders will have a website with information about their dogs and their policies; they also post litter announcements or future breeding plans in order to set up waiting lists of potential buyers for their puppies. A high quality, in demand breeder can have a waiting list that is over a year or two long, so it may take a while to be able to get your Malamute from them. But they are in demand for a good reason and these dogs are usually worth the wait, if you can be patient.

After they are born, puppies should remain with their mother and siblings for a minimum of 6-8 weeks, though 10-12 weeks is even better. This period gives the puppy the ability to speak and understand the complicated and subtle language of dogs. Puppies that are deprived of these vital lessons often grow up to be inexperienced in dog communication and body language and can sometimes become dog aggressive. They can get themselves or other dogs injured or even killed if the misunderstandings and poor communication get too out of hand.

Ethically and responsibly breeding dogs is no easy task. Good breeders maintain the highest standards of health, conformation, and temperament. They do not breed Malamutes for the money. In fact, good breeders often end up investing far more money into the puppies than they receive from their sale price. Health tests and numerous vet visits for both the bitch and her pups can get quite expensive, and that is just the beginning of what a responsible breeder pays for.

An ethical breeder only produces a small number of litters every year. Some will only breed their bitches 2-3 times in total. They take exceptional care of their Malamutes, treating them as beloved family members, and they are proud and eager to show them off to potential buyers, or anyone else. Beware of any breeder who is hesitant to show you their dogs or let you see where the puppies live. If they act like they may have something to hide, they very often do. It is best to avoid these types of breeders, as they care only about the money they will get and not about the dogs they are selling.

Most good breeders are quite selective about who they will sell their dogs to. Often, they have a detailed list of questions about you, your family, your house, and your lifestyle. They want to know as much as possible about you so they can best determine what type of owner you will be, and what your plans and intentions for their puppy may be. Since they care about their Malamutes, they care about where they go and what happens to them.

How to Interview Your Breeder

Once you find a potential breeder who interests you, interviewing them is the best way to find out the information you need to make the all-important decision of which puppy would be best for you and your family. The following questions will help you make that decision.

- Have both parents been health tested and certified by a veterinarian?
  - Many conditions and genetic disorders can be inherited from either parent. Having both parents tested and certified by a vet will let you know if your Malamute puppy is disease and disorder free.

Good breeders always have their dogs tested for multiple conditions to ensure that they produce the healthiest and highest quality puppies that they possibly can.

- Can you meet one or both parent dogs?
  - Carefully observe how the parents behave and interact with the puppies and their humans. Are they relaxed and friendly or tense, stressed, or anxious? Are they shy and fearful at all? Do they act dominant or aggressive in any way?
- How have the Malamute puppies been socialized?
  - Properly socializing the puppies within the first 6 months of their life is both necessary and crucial in establishing the foundation for future behaviors. Breeders should try to expose their puppies to as many new and different things as possible to give them the best chance of becoming healthy well-adjusted dogs as they grow up.
- What vaccinations have the Malamute puppies received?
  - How many have they had and when? What kind of shots did they receive? When is the next round due?
- Have they ever been examined and treated for worms?
  - Routine deworming is necessary since nearly all puppies are born with worms or parasites of some kind.
- Have any of the Malamute puppies ever been sick?
  - If so, what happened? What did the vet say? What sort of treatments were recommended? How effective were they against the illness? How long was the puppy sick for? Did they make a full recovery?
- Has the puppy ever been to see a vet before?
  - What did the vet say about them? Were any problems discovered? Have they ever been on any sort of medication before, and if so, what kind was it and what was it for?
- What sort of guarantee does the breeder have?
  - If the puppy develops an illness or condition, what is the breeder prepared to do? How long does the guarantee remain in effect after the purchase of the puppy?
- Is the breeder prepared to give you references and contact information for previous clients?

- Breeders should supply you with the contact information for at least two of their previous customers. Call and talk to them. Ask them how their experience with the breeder was. Were they completely satisfied with their Malamute? Did they have any problems or issues, and if so, what did the breeder do to resolve them? Would they ever consider buying another Malamute from them?

- Do they have a breeder's contract, and if so, what does it say?

  - What are the terms and stipulations listed in the contract? Does it have a spay and neuter clause? A return to breeder clause?

- What is the history of this specific line?

  - Ask to see the pedigree for the Malamutes. How far back does it go? How long did most of the Malamutes live? Did any have any major health problems? What did the dogs die from?

- What type of food are they currently using?

  - Continuing to feed the same food while gradually incorporating your own will reduce the chances of your Malamute suffering from gastrointestinal problems.

- Does the breeder supply a health guarantee or certificate along with a bill of sale?

- Is the breeder a member of any dog-oriented clubs?

  - Breed clubs, sports clubs, and training clubs are all excellent sources of information about the dog owner community. If the breeder is involved with a club, how long have they been a member? How active are they within the club?

- Do the Malamute parents have any titles? What about the grandparents?

- Are there any genetic defects or medical problems that commonly affect Malamutes?

- How long has the breeder been perfecting this line of Malamutes?

- Have they always worked with Malamutes or have they bred other breeds as well?

- What made them choose Malamutes?

Is the breeder willing to help find the perfect Malamute puppy for you, even if that requires recommending a different breeder, or even a different breed?

Professional breeders will likely be more than happy to answer all of your questions, offer advice, and help you in your quest to find a puppy. Be wary of any breeder who hesitates to answer your questions or seems reluctant to share information with you about themselves or their dogs. The more questions you ask, the more you can learn, and the more prepared you become to find your perfect companion.

Breeder Contracts

A lot of breeders require buyers to sign a contract. It outlines very specifically what is and is not acceptable to do to or with the dog. The average contract defines the payment amount for the Malamute puppy and has terms or rules for what happens if you can no longer keep the dog. Most breeders demand that their Malamute be returned to them if you can no longer provide a home for him, rather than giving the dog to a rescue or surrendering it to the animal shelter.

Some breeder contracts also require that you spay or neuter your dog. There will often be a time requirement for this. As more research comes out, breeders are more often stipulating that you wait until after the dog is fully mature, between 12 and 18 months old, before sterilizing. This is said to help prevent certain diseases including bone cancer, in the future.

A good breeder will always guarantee the health of their puppies in the contract. Look for guarantees that will refund most or all of the cost of the puppy in the event that any congenital health conditions appear within the first year. Beware of breeders who only offer to replace the puppy with a healthy one, with no option to receive a refund instead. If the breeder produced a genetically unhealthy puppy the first time, why would you want to bring home another puppy from the same place? Many people are also unwilling to return their dog for a replacement as they have already become attached. This is a low-risk guarantee from a breeder and may be a warning sign. On the other hand, a responsible breeder will always take back a dog that you can no longer care for, no matter the reason.

Remember, no matter how good the breeding lines are or how thorough the testing, a puppy is a living creature and diseases can develop. No breeder can guarantee perfect health for a dog's entire life.

A lot of breeders require that potential buyers, their families and whatever pets they may have, meet the puppy they are interested in buying before taking them home to ensure that everyone gets along and that the Malamute is compatible with the family before letting him go to his new home. Some breeders even require a home check where they come out to view your house to verify that everything is as it should be, and that all the needs of the Malamute will be met and that he will be safe and properly taken care of.

Good breeders are also more than happy to offer advice to new owners and help them out with whatever problems or behavior issues that come up over the course of the dog's life. They also prefer that owners stay connected and give them the occasional update, so they know how their Malamutes are doing throughout their lives.

Importance of Breeder Reputation

Finding a trustworthy breeder can be a challenge when there are so many questionable breeders out there. People will pay good money for a purebred dog and this has caused many to take up "backyard breeding." Oftentimes these breeders do little or no testing to ensure the health of their litters. Some of these places even turn out to be puppy mills. These are places where dogs are kept alive to do nothing more than pump out litter after litter. Often kept in small cages in unclean conditions, this is a terrible life for a dog! Avoiding supporting places like this is just as important as ensuring the health of your puppy.

A good, reputable breeder will be known as such in the Alaskan Malamute breeder community. They will undoubtedly have connections with other reputable breeders. If you find a good breeder who has no current available puppies, you may want to contact them and ask for the names of other breeders in the area. A reputable breeder is always concerned with breeding dogs up to the standard of the breed and should only recommend the same.

Choosing Your Pick of the Litter

"Choosing the right Malamute for your family has a lot to do with the people involved in the process, as well as Malamute. Don't just choose a puppy based on a cute photo you have seen online, call and ask questions and then go for a visit."

Gail Partain
Windwalker Malamutes

Once you have found a reputable breeder from which to purchase your Alaskan Malamute, the day will soon come to choose your new puppy from the litter!

Although temperament and behavior characteristics should be relatively consistent throughout a well-bred litter of Malamutes, individual puppy personalities will vary. If possible, visit your breeder's facility before take home day to pick out your new puppy.

If you are able to visit the litter beforehand, there are a few things to keep in mind. If the puppies are all playing together, does one seem more aggressive than another? This one may be feisty, energetic, and a bit more assertive by nature. Is there one who would rather play alone in the corner with her own toy? This puppy may be a bit more docile and independent. Is there one that is climbing all over you, gnawing on your hands or shoes? This could be a puppy with a naturally more curious and adventurous personality. None of these personalities are better or worse than the other, but you should have a type of dog in mind that you are hoping for so that you can make the best choice for your family and for your future puppy.

If you are unsure which puppy you should choose, ask the breeder for help. They are the ones who have spent the most time with the puppies and should have a pretty good idea of each of their personalities.

The Different Puppy Personality Types

"If possible, interact with the pup's parents. Are they friendly? Do they shy away from people? Do they growl at people? The pups observe and learn from their parent's fears and/or eagerness to meet new people."

Randy Checketts
Chex Alaskan Malamutes

Most puppies will fit into 1 of 5 categories.

The Dominant Puppy
This puppy will be bossy, pushy, and probably more vocal than the others. He might be rebellious and particularly challenging to train, generally requiring a strong and experienced leader to keep him in line. These puppies can sometimes have aggression and behavior problems later in life unless they are handled correctly and carefully.

Signs of a Dominant Puppy
- Mounts or climbs on siblings, or leans heavily on them
- Steals food, treats, toys, or attention
- Plays rough and is usually overly growly
- Can be excessively mouthy and likes to bite, especially while playing

The Active Puppy

These puppies can also be pushy and bossy to an extent, and can sometimes be overly mouthy. They are usually very high-energy dogs that get excited very easily. They lose focus quickly and are easily distracted, which can make training quite difficult. These puppies will require an owner who remains calm and does not get frustrated or upset and has a lot of patience. These dogs will need a good amount of exercise and mental stimulation to avoid becoming bored. They require consistent repetitive training and usually need a firm, experienced leader to properly guide them.

Signs of an Independent Puppy

- Happy playing by himself and may remove himself purposefully from the group or stay away from siblings
- Will defend what he has, but will rarely try to take anything away from someone else
- Not obviously submissive or dominant, instead falling somewhere in the middle
- Mostly calm and quiet, content to remain off to the side and watch the others play
- Tends to stay close to mom or in the middle of the puppy pack, avoiding being near the edge or alone.

The Affectionate Puppy

These puppies are incredibly friendly and always eager to please. They usually learn new things rather quickly and are usually easier to train than other types of dogs. They are quite outgoing and have a good amount of self-confidence, sure of their place within the world. They are a wonderful choice for families with children and tend to form extraordinarily strong bonds quickly with their humans. They generally get along well with other dogs and animals and are more accepting of other pets than the other personality types. These dogs will need a lot of love and attention, and they are always happiest when they are near their people.

The Calm Puppy

More submissive than other personality types and happy to be a follower, not a leader, these puppies are more laid back and mellow, with lower energy levels than their siblings, so they do not require as much exercise or work. They are usually quite affectionate dogs, believing that they are "lap dogs" and are more than delighted to curl up with you on the couch for a long snuggle. They are mostly eager to please but sometimes require more work to build motivation during training sessions. They are mostly friendly and get along well with other dogs and animals. However, they can require a great deal of time and attention and can be prone to separation anxiety when left alone.

Signs of a Docile Puppy

- Not pushy or overly fearful; tends toward more of a middle-type personality

- Likes to interact with siblings and is quite friendly and playful

- Tries to avoid fights and does not tend to steal toys or treats from the others

- Shows submission to more dominant puppies, but does not exert dominance over more submissive puppies

The Fearful Puppy

Highly submissive dogs, these puppies can be quite shy and timid at times and are easily scared or intimidated. They lack self-confidence, can be quite sensitive, and can easily have their feelings hurt. They are usually scared of or intimidated by anything new or unusual – people, places, other animals, anything really – and require a high amount of work and socialization to be able to adjust and get used to the world around them. They do best when they have a calm and quiet owner who has a great deal of compassion and patience, and who has a gentle, understanding training style. Loud noises, punishment, and even light corrections may be too much for these dogs to handle. A reputable Malamute breeder should not have any "fearful" puppies in a healthy litter. If you notice there are fearful puppies among the litter, it may be a red flag that something is wrong.

Signs of a Submissive Puppy

- Easily pushed around and constantly picked on by siblings

- Often pushed out of the group and excluded from games and play time

- When conflict arises, quick to flip on his back, exposing his tummy in submission

- Gives up toys or treats quickly if challenged for them

- Prefers to stick close to mother, both for protection and for comfort

Tests for Evaluating Your Malamute Puppy

"When choosing a pup from a breeder, it is important to tell the breeder what kind of home environment the pup will be living in so they (the breeder) can fit the pup to the family. Thus, do not choose a pup based on its color, choose on temperament and health. Let the breeder help you choose which pup is right for your family and life style."

Laurie Knight
Tall Timber Malamutes

Photo Courtesy of Phyllis Albertson

There are a variety of different tests you can do to get a good sense of what your puppy's future personality and natural reactions will be like. It is best to assess each puppy individually, away from the influence of the rest of the pack. Take the puppy several feet away from its littermate before starting your tests.

Behavior Test #1

Firmly and fully stroke the puppy from his head down to his tail, exerting a gentle but firm pressure.

- Dominant Puppies – ,Will not like this action and will either try to struggle and escape, or may alternatively jump towards you, paw at you or try to nip or bite you, possibly while growling.

- Submissive Puppies – Will try to lick at your face or hands, squirm a bit, and try to roll over and expose their tummy, submitting to your authority and dominance over them.

- Independent Puppies – Generally will either try to calmly move away and put distance between you and them, or they will "freeze" and become tense and stiff, not moving at all.

- Docile Puppies – Get wiggly and whine or freeze like their more independent siblings. But this usually passes quickly, and they will settle down and relax, either trying to lick your hands or scoot closer to you for contact and comfort.

Behavior Test #2

Pick up each puppy in turn, holding it upside down like a baby. Gently but firmly place your hand on each puppy's chest while maintaining non-threatening eye contact.

- Dominant Puppies – Will squirm or wiggle, trying to escape your hold on them, and tend to either growl at you or try to nip or bite at you if they can.

- Submissive Puppies – Will become wriggly and squirmy if they are intimidated, or they will try to lick your hands if not. They will occasionally return eye contact, though not steadily.

- Independent Puppies – Will only struggle briefly, if at all, but soon give up. They will most likely avoid returning your eye contact, keeping their gaze steadily elsewhere, any-where but at you.

- Docile Puppies – Will not try to escape or object to your han-dling for very long before they relax and accept your em-brace, as unusual and strange as it may be. Your constant gentle eye contact may have a calming effect on them.

Behavior Test #3

Place your hands underneath each puppy's tummy and lift its paws completely off the ground for 30 seconds. Hold the puppy gently, but firm-ly, making sure that it is steady and balanced in your hands.

- Dominant Puppies – Will keep struggling against your hold, twisting, and trying to nip or bite at you, usually growling the whole time or most of the time.

- Submissive Puppies – Will tend to accept this hold with lit-tle or no fuss or struggle, but they may try to twist a bit in your grip in an attempt to lick at your hands or any other part that they can reach.

- Independent Puppies – Will most likely freeze, offering lit-tle or no resistance at all, but clearly not enjoying or ac-cepting your grasp either.

- Docile Puppies – Will wriggle and squirm a little at first, but quickly relax and settle down, possibly attempting to lick at your hands if they can reach them.

Testing Social Behavior Test #1

Put each puppy on the ground and let it do its own thing for 30-60 sec-onds or so. When the puppy is clearly not paying any attention to you any-more, crouch down and encourage it to come to you with a combination of calls, kissy sounds, soft hand claps, or whatever else seems to work.

- Dominant Puppies – Will most likely come to you right away, possibly at a run. Once they reach you, they will try to jump up onto you, paw at you, or nip/bite at your hands or pants, or whatever else they can manage to reach.

- Submissive Puppies –Will most likely need a lot more en-couragement and motivation to get them to actually come to you, and when they do come closer to you, it may be in a submissive posture, "creeping" or crawling along on their bellies. They may even urinate when they get close enough to you, in a clear sign of fear and submission. They are obviously very anxious and agitated.

- Independent Puppies – Probably will not be interested in coming to you. If they do come to you, they will only do so in their own time, when they feel like it, not because you called them. Either that or they will ignore you entirely, and possibly wander off in a different direction.

- Docile Puppies – Will happily come quickly to you, though not as quickly as the dominant type puppies did. They will be happy and excited, trying to lick at your hands and face, and whatever else they can reach, but they will not be overly pushy about anything.

Testing Social Behavior Test #2

Crouch down and talk to each puppy while petting it for a long moment, then calmly and quietly get up and start to walk away. Do not encourage the puppy to follow, look back, or make any noise towards the puppy at all. Ignore it completely.

- Dominant Puppies – Will be inclined to race after you in a hurry, winding and running around your legs, biting at your ankles and the bottoms of your pants, your shoelaces, and generally making a complete nuisance of themselves.

- Submissive Puppies – Will probably stop and think for a moment or two, then probably follow after you, albeit slowly. They may catch up to you, but most likely they will stay a few feet behind you, just in case...

- Independent Puppies –Probably will show no interest at all in following after you. They are more likely to turn around and wander off in another direction to explore by themselves than follow after you and your foolishness.

- Docile Puppies – Will most likely scamper after you right away, quickly catching up with and walking with you, may attempt to paw at you or get your attention somehow, but they won't be pushy about it like the dominant puppies were.

CHAPTER 3
Preparing for Your New Malamute

Pre-Puppy Preparation

The more prepared you are for your Malamute's arrival, the smoother and easier the transition will be, and the quicker your puppy will adjust to its new life.

Photo Courtesy of Nathan Martin

Rules and Routines

"I tell everyone, grow them like you want them to be when they are grown. If you let your puppy on the bed or sofa now, then the puppy is going to expect to be able to get on the bed or sofa when he or she is grown."

Gail Partain
Windwalker Malamutes

This is one of the most important parts of your young Malamute's life. Rules should be discussed with the entire family and decided on before the puppy arrives. It is particularly important that everyone in the household is on the same page and follows and reinforces the same rules. This avoids confusion and helps to make sure that everything remains consistent for your Malamute. The more consistent everything is, the faster your puppy will learn the rules

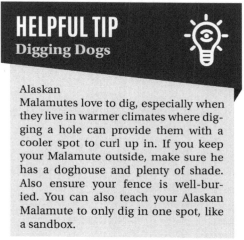

HELPFUL TIP
Digging Dogs

Alaskan Malamutes love to dig, especially when they live in warmer climates where digging a hole can provide them with a cooler spot to curl up in. If you keep your Malamute outside, make sure he has a doghouse and plenty of shade. Also ensure your fence is well-buried. You can also teach your Alaskan Malamute to only dig in one spot, like a sandbox.

and what is expected. If everyone follows and enforces the same rules, it will set your puppy up for success while minimizing accidents and failures.

Some of the rules your family should discuss include:

Q: Will the Malamute be allowed on furniture?
A: This varies from household to household. Some people do not mind their dog climbing up on the couch or into bed with them and other people are strictly opposed.

Q: Where will the Malamute be sleeping? What will it be sleeping in?
A: In the beginning, your Malamute will need to sleep in a crate while being trained. Where will this crate be kept? Taking care of a young puppy can be much like caring for a baby, so your Malamute should be kept close by during the night for easy bathroom outings.

Q: Who will be in charge of feeding? When will your young Malamute be fed each day and how much should he eat? What sort of food will you use?

A: It is better if one person oversees the feedings, though this is not always possible. An adult should always be in charge of this responsibility, though you can have children assist you if you like. It is important that you teach children to stay away from your Malamute while he is eating.

Q: Who will be responsible for walking the Malamute each day? How many times a day will he be walked and at what times? How long will he be walked for and on which routes?

A: A child should never be allowed to walk a Malamute by themselves without adult supervision. The pup will only need short walks at first but as he grows older and his exercise needs grow, your Malamute will need much longer, more vigorous walks. Eventually, a long daily walk will no longer be enough exercise for a Malamute that lives inside a house.

Most people who own Malamutes are invested in a sport of some kind, and there are a lot of different activities that you can do with your Malamute, like dogsledding, weight-pulling, carting, and many other things. These will be more fully discussed in a further chapter.

Q: How will training be done? What will the Malamute be trained for? What commands will be used for what actions?

A: Decide whether or not your Malamute will attend training classes. Make a list of commands that everyone agrees to use and hang it somewhere prominent in the house where it will be seen frequently, like on the refrigerator. Add new commands to the list as training progresses and as your Malamute learns new words. Before you know it, he will know pages of commands!

Q: How will corrections be handled?

A: Never hit or kick your dog. Hitting your dog is never acceptable and will not correct the unwanted behavior. Redirection is much more effective and will help cultivate the bond of trust between you and your Malamute.

Q: Who will clean up after the dog? Who will be in charge of cleaning up the yard every week? Who will be cleaning up accidents? Who will clean the crate and the food bowls?

A: It may be best to make a list of weekly chores related to the Malamute and have a rotating schedule so that everyone ends up helping out with the not-so-fun part of caring for a dog. Another option is to place one person in charge of one specific chore, such as mom cleans the crate; dad cleans the yard, etc.

Preparing Your Home

Along with getting your family ready for the Malamute's homecoming, you will want to also prepare your home. Puppy proofing will ensure that your Malamute will be coming into a safe environment.

Puppy-Proofing Your Home

"Puppy proofing a home can often be trial and error as it depends on the personality of the puppy. What works for one might not work for another. I recommend getting down on the ground and trying to think like a puppy. They like small dark places where they can curl up and they will chew on everything."

Brian Trujillo
Trujillo's Malamutes

One of the first things you should do in preparation for your new Malamute is to puppy-proof your home. There are many seemingly ordinary things in your home that could prove hazardous to the new addition to the family.

1. **Hide or remove any electrical cords within the puppy's reach.** Puppies are curious little creatures who love to explore, oftentimes with their mouths. If you cannot remove the cords from your puppy's reach, you may want to invest in some cord protectors. These cord wraps usually come infused with bitter flavors to help deter chewing. If you find you have a particularly stubborn chewer, you can spritz the cords with no-chew spray, found in pet stores, to ensure he will not find the cord appealing anymore.

Photo Courtesy of
Amanda Nuckoles

2. **Invest in fully enclosed trash cans if you do not have them already.**
Keeping the kitchen trash out of reach may be a no brainer but even the smaller trash cans around your bathrooms and office are tempting playthings for a small, curious Malamute puppy. Sometimes a used cotton swab or a wad of paper is just too irresistible not to chew up.

3. **Put up all medications, chemicals, and cleaning supplies.**
If you tend to keep any medications in an area that your puppy may be able to reach, be sure to move those to a higher location, such as a dedicated medicine cabinet. As mentioned above, puppies explore everything with their mouths and snatching a bottle or box of medication off the sofa table could prove to be fatal for your new puppy. Also, move any chemicals, cleaning supplies, dish pods, or laundry detergents into an enclosed area and out of reach. This includes any rat bait or poisons that your new puppy may find enticing. Even if you think these items are in an area of the house your puppy will not be allowed, it only takes one escape for your new Malamute to encounter something detrimental.

4. **Watch out for poisonous house plants.**
House plants may seem innocent but not all are the same. Some houseplants are actually poisonous and can cause serious issues for a nibbling puppy. Some of the most common houseplants that are potentially dangerous for your new puppy are the Corn Plant, Sago Palm, Aloe, and Jade Plant. To find a complete list, visit the ASPCA website.

5. **Beware of xylitol.**
Xylitol is considered a sugar alcohol and is commonly found in items throughout almost every household. As people become more and more

Photo Courtesy of
Doris Thompson

aware of the dangers of added sugars, companies are turning to xylitol, an additive that tastes sweet but does not spike blood sugar and insulin levels like sugar. Xylitol can be found in almost anything, but is most commonly found in chewing gum, mints, candies, toothpaste, and even peanut butter. Xylitol is highly toxic to dogs and can cause dangerously low blood sugar levels resulting in weakness, seizures, trembling, or even death. When dogs consume very high levels of xylitol, it may cause necrosis of the liver which often leads to death.

Be sure to keep all purses and bags which may contain gum, candies, or toothpaste up and out of reach of your puppy at all times. Have a designated area for guests' bags so they are not accidentally left within reach. Also, check all food labels for xylitol before giving your puppy a special treat. It is often recommended to give a dog peanut butter to help him take any medication, but be sure to check that your peanut butter does not contain xylitol first.

6. **Keep the batteries away.**
   While you probably don't have random batteries lying around on the floor, you may have remotes or small electronic toys. If your puppy is able to get ahold of a battery operated remote or toy, he could potentially chew them enough to expose the battery. Small button cell batteries are the most dangerous as they are small enough for your puppy to swallow. Swallowing a battery is a serious, life-threatening issue and can cause internal burns. Call the nearest emergency vet immediately if you suspect your puppy may have swallowed a battery.

7. **Put away any children's toys.**
   Children's toys are often made up of small pieces that are a choking hazard to your dog. Be especially careful with toys that contain magnets inside as these pose an extra risk of internal damage when more than one is consumed.

8. **Set up puppy gates.**
   After you have puppy-proofed your entire house, you should designate a safe common area for your puppy to stay. Use puppy gates to block any doorways or staircases so it will be easier for you to keep a close eye on your new Malamute. Having already puppy-proofed the entire house, you can be sure that even if your Malamute ventures into a room he is not allowed, the dangerous items have all been removed.

It only takes one second for your new Malamute to get into something that could cause him harm, so it is extremely important you notify everyone in the house of the changes being made before your puppy comes home.

Photo Courtesy of
Amanda Lafave

Dangerous Things Your Dog Might Eat

Although feeding your dog food from the table is not recommended, it's often difficult to resist those begging eyes looking up at you while you eat. If you do get the urge to toss your pup a little treat, make sure you know what he can and can't have. There are a number of foods, perfectly healthy for humans, that can and do cause illness or toxicity in dogs.

Chocolate – A crowd favorite among humans, chocolate can cause major issues for your Malamute. Chocolate contains methylxanthines, which are a stimulant that can stop a dog's metabolic process. Methylxanthines are found in especially high amounts in pure dark chocolate and bakers chocolate. Consuming too much methylxanthine causes seizures and irregular heart function which can lead to death.

Xylitol – As discussed before, xylitol is particularly dangerous to dogs as it does not take much to cause a dangerous or deadly reaction. Vomiting is typically the initial symptom of xylitol poisoning. If you suspect there is a chance your dog has ingested even a small amount of xylitol, call the veterinarian immediately because time is critical.

Raw or Cooked Bones – Raw or cooked bones are a choking hazard for your dog. The bones can break or splinter and become lodged or worse, puncture a dog's digestive tract. This is especially true with cooked bones of any kind as they become dry and brittle. Pork and poultry bones are especially dangerous as they are more likely to splinter and cause issues.

Though controversial, some veterinarians say that raw bones of the right variety can provide healthy nutrients and help prevent tartar and plaque build-up in the mouth. These bones are recommended only under very close supervision and only for a few minutes at a time, placing the bone in the refrigerator for a maximum of four days before discarding. If the bone is breaking or if your dog seems to be swallowing any pieces, discard the bone immediately. If you prefer to skip the risk, look for bones in the pet store that are meant to withstand heavy chewing without breaking.

Other foods that may cause gastrointestinal upset or worse for your dog are grapes and raisins, certain nuts including macadamia nuts, avocados, apple cores and seeds, and anything in the allium family including onions and garlic. This is not a comprehensive list so it is best to check with your veterinarian before giving anything from your plate to your dog.

Photo Courtesy of
Sarah Schmidt

Preparing an Outdoor Space

Alaskan Malamutes were bred to work and work hard. They have high exercise needs and will not be happy laying around a house all day. Letting your Malamute exert some energy in the backyard is a great way to keep him healthy and occupied but be sure to take all necessary precautions beforehand to keep your dog safe.

Start preparing your outdoor space ahead of time by removing all chemical products from the area. Any weed or pest killers, fertilizers, or other similar products should be placed somewhere the dog cannot reach. Your garage should also be puppy-proofed. Put up any toxic chemicals such as anti-freeze or paint cans.

If you plan to allow your Malamute to play unsupervised for any period of time, you will need to be sure the yard is secure. Check all fencing to be sure there are no gaps between the fence and the ground. Make sure all gates latch completely and there is no way for your Malamute to climb or jump over the fence. You will need a minimum of a 6 foot fence that is either buried in the ground or set in concrete. Malamutes are curious and independent and will take any opportunity to escape for an adventure. Always be sure your Malamute is wearing his collar and tags before allowing him outside for any amount of time. You will also want to make sure your Malamute has a shady spot to cool off in the summer heat and a constant water source.

Just like with indoor plants, some outdoor plants and flowers can prove to be poisonous to your dog. Check the list again against any plants you may have in your garden and replace those that may be harmful with a safe alternative.

Preparing Children and Other Pets

If you are bringing your new puppy home to a house with no children or other pets, the transition should be a relatively easy one. If you do have children or other pets, you must make careful preparations to allow everyone time to adjust. In regards to children, depending on their age, the only preparations needed will be to teach them gentle handling of your future puppy. Most children are excited and cannot wait to get their new puppy, so adjusting them to the idea should be a breeze. Even Malamute puppies are delicate at a young age, so it is especially important to show children how to safely hold, pick up, and pet your puppy. Often, a small child can harm a puppy unintentionally by trying to show affection in a manner too rough. Careful supervision should be maintained with small children and puppies, even if you think they understand.

When it comes to adjusting your current pets to the idea of a new puppy, things may get a little more complicated. Depending on the type of pets and their nature, the transition may be simple or it may take a little extra work. While Malamutes typically do not get along with other dogs well, introducing him as a puppy may help him bond and adjust, preventing future issues.

If you have another dog or multiple dogs, warming them up to the idea of a new puppy before the introduction is a good idea. Discuss this transition with your chosen breeder and see if they will allow you to pick up a blanket or a toy with the new puppy's scent on it. Introduce the blanket or toy to your current dog or dogs and allow them to become accustomed to the smell of another puppy in the house.

When you pick up your new puppy, have someone help you with the first introduction. If possible, let your dogs meet your new puppy in a neutral area where your current pets will be less likely to be territorial. Because your puppy's immune system is not fully developed, you will not want to take your new puppy to a park or another public place, but you may consider letting them meet briefly outside of the house in a less used area. Keep your dogs leashed but give them a bit of slack so they can greet the puppy. Keep a close eye on all parties during the introduction to ensure the safety of your new puppy. Keep the first meeting brief and then separate your dogs from the new puppy so they do not overwhelm each other. After you see how they react to each other, you can slowly allow them to spend more time together until they are completely acclimated and coexisting in harmony.

If you are introducing your puppy to a resident cat, it's important to keep both your cat and puppy safe by maintaining control of your puppy or by allowing them to meet while one animal is contained by a crate or another barrier. Allow them short, controlled interactions at quiet moments of the day until they are both calm around each other.

A new puppy can be exciting and become the focal point of life for a while. Remember to show your other dogs and pets some extra attention and love so they know that they are still important members of the family.

Supplies to Purchase Before You Bring Your Malamute Home

Getting ready for a new puppy can be overwhelming. There is so much information to learn and so many preparations to be made around the house. Gathering all the supplies you need before you bring your puppy home will make the first few days much easier. Follow this list of essentials and you will have all you need for the day you bring your Malamute home.

Food and water bowl – Food and water bowls come in many shapes, colors, and sizes. They can be made from ceramic, stainless steel, or plastic. When choosing a bowl set for your new puppy, there are a few things to consider. Plastic bowls may come in fun colors and patterns but they are lightweight, easy to tip over, and many puppies think they are fun to chew on. They are also more difficult to clean thoroughly when they become scratched or damaged.

Ceramic bowls are heavier, less likely to be tipped over, and are easier to clean than plastic. They are breakable, though, so as your Malamute grows he may manage to knock it over and move it around, likely breaking it.

Stainless-steel bowls are both easy to clean and unbreakable so even if they are tipped over and kicked around, they shouldn't get damaged. You can also buy these bowls with wide rubber or silicone bases to stop sliding and prevent tipping.

Another option you will find in a pet store is an elevated bowl set. These are bowls that are set up off the floor so that your dog doesn't have to bend over as far to eat. Created to try to help prevent the serious issue of bloat in some breeds, studies have actually shown that elevated feeders can potentially contribute to bloat. If you are adopting an older Malamute that has neck or mobility issues, then an elevated dog feeder would be something to discuss with your veterinarian as an option.

Collar, tags, and leash – One of the first things you will want to do when you get your new puppy is put on his collar with identification tags. These tags can be made at any local pet store or you can order one from an online retailer. It's best to always have your pet's name, your current address, and phone number on the tag. This is meant to help a stranger return your dog in the event he ever gets lost. You can even add a little note that says "Please Call My Family."

Food – Your breeder should send a small amount of food home with your puppy to get you through the first couple of days. It would be best to continue with this same brand of food as it is probably a high-quality brand and will save your puppy any intestinal upset from switching. If you do want to switch foods, talk with your breeder about how to do it safely. They will probably recommend you switch gradually by mixing in the puppy's current food with the new food over a period of a several days.

Puppy-safe toys – Your puppy will have lots of energy and very sharp teeth. In order to save your couch legs and your shoes, you will want to have at least four or five different dog toys for your puppy to choose from. Because you do not yet know what your puppy will prefer, get at least one plush toy, one rubber toy or bone, one rope, and one ball. Buy toys with different squeaker sounds and textures to see which one your puppy will love the most. You may find that plush toys don't last long before being ripped to shreds or you may find that your new puppy loves carrying that stuffed elephant all around the house!

Grooming brush – Alaskan Malamutes have thick, fluffy double coats and require frequent brushing to keep them from shedding everywhere.

Puppy training treats – To help with potty training and teaching basic commands, it is essential to have a bag of treats. Look for soft treats that

are healthy and natural. Be sure that they contain no animal byproduct, are grain-free, and have no artificial flavors, colors, or preservatives.

Crate and pad – Your puppy will need somewhere safe to stay while you are gone or when you can't keep a close eye on him, such as at night. Invest in a quality crate and pad that will be big enough for your fully grown Malamute and establish it as a safe place early on in the training process. It's ideal to buy a crate pad that is washable and has minimal stuffing because chances are, it will be chewed on at some point.

You will need to invest in a crate that is large enough for an adult Malamute so that you can continue use as he grows. For a young puppy of 10 or 12 weeks, you may want to use a divider to cut down your puppy's space to an area that's just big enough for him to turn around and lie down. If a puppy has too much space, he may urinate or defecate inside the crate, setting back his housetraining significantly.

Puppy gate or play pen – You will not want your new puppy to have full range of the house right off the bat. Unless your space allows you to keep your puppy contained in a centralized location, you will probably want to purchase a puppy gate or playpen. The idea is to give your young Malamute his own designated "safe space" where he can play without constant supervision. A gate that blocks a doorway is a good way to keep your puppy from venturing down a hall, up the stairs, or into a room that is off limits, but it still allows him access to furniture or other things in an area which could potentially become chew things. A play pen allows much more flexibility as you can move it around wherever inside or outside of the house you will be. A play pen also keeps any furniture from becoming damaged by those razor-sharp puppy teeth.

CHAPTER 4
Bringing Your Malamute Home

There is nothing more exciting than the day you get to pick up your new Malamute from the breeder! You've done your research, prepared your home and yard, purchased all the needed supplies, and now all that's left is to bring your puppy home. You may find yourself a bit anxious, wondering how everything will go, but if you follow the tips below, pick-up day should be fun, exciting, and trouble free.

*Photo Courtesy of
Dawn Hanmore*

Picking Up Your Malamute

When you arrive at the breeding facility at your appointed time, your breeder should have the puppy ready to go in a designated pick-up area. He may be in a pen playing with other puppies that are leaving on the same day. Try not to let the adorable sight of your new Malamute keep you from hearing the important information your breeder will give you!

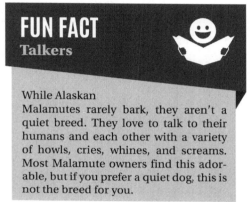

FUN FACT
Talkers

While Alaskan Malamutes rarely bark, they aren't a quiet breed. They love to talk to their humans and each other with a variety of howls, cries, whines, and screams. Most Malamute owners find this adorable, but if you prefer a quiet dog, this is not the breed for you.

Before you leave, your breeder should give you detailed information on your puppy's vet records, current shots, future shots, and dewormings. They should remind you of any stipulations of the health guarantee and advise you on a feeding schedule. All of this information as well as breed-specific care tips should be neatly presented in a packet of some sort along with registration papers.

Sometimes a breeder will allow you to take a small blanket or toy home with your dog so that the smell of his litter can comfort him during the transition. It may be beneficial to ask ahead of time if this is an option in order to know if you need to provide the blanket before pick-up day.

The Ride Home

Depending on how far you have to travel to pick up your Malamute, you will want to plan accordingly. It's not uncommon for a puppy to get motion sick and vomit on the ride home, so you may consider requesting that the breeder withhold food for that morning. Regardless of how long the trip is, you will want to be sure to take a bowl and a bottle of water for your puppy in the case of an unexpected delay, like a flat tire.

There are a couple of options when it comes to transporting your new Malamute. Some people let the puppy ride home in a crate. If you plan to transport the puppy in the crate, place only towels in the bottom of the crate so the crate pad is not soiled on the trip. Also, take care to drive extra smoothly so you do not jostle your puppy any more than necessary.

Not all crates will withstand the force of a crash and some can even become more dangerous for your dog in the event of a crash. When not properly secured to the vehicle, the crate can become a projectile, injuring your puppy and possibly other passengers in the car. You can visit the Center for Pet Safety (CPS) website for a list of tested and approved travel crates.

If you are thinking of buying a harness for your dog to use in the car, know that they are not all created equally. The Center for Pet Safety performed a Harness Crashworthiness Study in 2013 and results showed that only one of eleven brands tested performed at the level advertised. Some were even deemed "catastrophic failures." Do diligent research on each brand before making your decision.

Don't be tempted to let the puppy ride in your lap. This is very dangerous for your dog. In the event of a crash, the puppy can be killed by the airbag or become a projectile. Even breaking too hard can cause injury to your puppy if he or she is not secured.

Before beginning the journey home, allow your puppy to use the restroom on a patch of grass. Praise him if he does and then begin your trip home. The ride home can be a great bonding opportunity for you and your puppy, so enjoy those first moments together as a new family.

Photo Courtesy of Brooke Hanley

Photo Courtesy of
Jennifer Diavolitsis

Your Malamute's First Night

"Puppies like to chew and one of the things they go after first are cords. Make sure they cannot get to any TV, lamp, or phone recharging cords."

Randy Checketts
Chex Alaskan Malamutes

Before bed, take your Malamute outside and wait 10 to 15 minutes for him to relieve himself. If he doesn't go, wait ten minutes and then try again. Repeat this process for however long it takes your puppy to go and then put him directly into the crate for bed with his special blanket or toy from the breeder. It may be helpful for nighttime bathroom outings if you keep the crate by your bed.

The first night home can be daunting and scary for both you and your puppy. That crate can look awfully lonely and uncomfortable for your new Malamute. He is not accustomed to sleeping alone so there will probably be a lot of whining and crying for the first few nights. After all, this will be the very first time your puppy has spent the night away from mom and siblings. Although it will be tempting to pull your puppy out of the crate and let him sleep with you, it would be best for everyone if you resist the urge and allow your puppy to self-soothe in the crate.

Remember that your puppy will probably need to be taken outside to relieve himself at least once during the night. If your puppy wakes you in the

Photo Courtesy of
Shay Wilhite

night, it's best to take him outside and then immediately return him right back to the crate to sleep. This will teach him that nighttime is for sleeping and not for playing.

If your puppy is having a difficult time sleeping in the crate or is keeping you awake with his crying, try talking to your puppy or rubbing his head through the crate to help calm him. You may even try shushing him like you would a baby. The most important thing you can do in the first few days is to make your puppy feel loved and secure. Bonds you form with each other in the early days will last throughout your dog's lifetime and will make all aspects of dog ownership that much more enjoyable.

After a few nights, the bedtime whining should stop and your puppy should come to find his crate a cozy place to sleep. As you and your puppy both adjust to life with each other, routines will form and things will get much easier.

Choosing the Right Veterinarian

When searching for the perfect veterinarian for your new Malamute, you may be tempted to go online and read reviews. Beware that not all reviews are an accurate depiction of an establishment. Animals are beloved by their owners and sometimes unfavorable things happen that are out of the veterinarian's control. It is very easy for a heartbroken owner to take to the internet and blame the vet for their unfortunate circumstances when the vet may have had nothing to do with the outcome. Instead, start with word of mouth. Ask fellow dog owners which vet they prefer and which ones they would avoid. Make a list of the most favorable and start with those.

Next, eliminate some off your list based on location. In an emergency, you will want to have chosen a vet that is nearby. If there are any clinics on your list that you feel are too far in the event of a crisis, cross them off.

Call all the remaining clinics on your list and inquire about their prices. You can get a good comparison by asking what they charge for a round of shots, a spay or neuter, and an x-ray. Make notes of what each clinic charges and how they accept payment. Do they demand it all upfront or do they offer payment plans? Also make note of the friendliness of the office staff when you call. Did they offer the information willingly or seem put out? You don't want to commit to a vet clinic with unhelpful office staff. That could make any visit an unpleasant experience.

You should also ask about the prospective vet's policy in regard to vaccinations. The American Animal Hospital Association's current guidelines

Photo Courtesy of
Danielle Court

recommend that core vaccines (distemper/parvo/parainfluenza/adenovirus and rabies), after the initial puppy shots and 1 year booster, be given no more often than every 3 years. Make certain that the vet you choose is aware of these guidelines, and does not insist on vaccinating every year throughout the dog's life. Non-core vaccines (Bordetella, leptospirosis, Lyme) should only be given when warranted; a good vet will help you determine whether or not these vaccines are appropriate for your Malamute's lifestyle and circumstances.

If after all of the above steps you still haven't decided, call each clinic and ask to make an appointment to visit in person. While on your visits, ask the staff or the vet if they have any other Alaskan Malamutes as patients or have experience with the breed. You will likely find that one of the offices is a better fit for you and your puppy than the others and your decision will be easy. It is important to trust your veterinarian and feel comfortable in their clinic, so don't settle on a vet without taking all the necessary steps.

The First Vet Visit

Some breeders stipulate that you must take your puppy to the vet within a few days for a check-up. If this is the case, you'll want to call and make an appointment with your chosen vet before you pick up your puppy. Be sure to take all records given to you by the breeder for the vet to include in your Malamute's file.

The first appointment will typically be a general look over to make sure your puppy is in good health. Your puppy will be weighed and the vet will examine eyes, ears, nose, heart, and lungs. They will look at your dog's skin and coat condition and examine the teeth and mouth. They may take a stool sample to check for parasites. If it's time for your puppy's next round of shots, they will get them at this appointment.

This appointment should be relatively quick and easy. Take this opportunity to ask your vet any questions you may have about feeding or caring for your new puppy. If you have made a list of questions, don't be afraid to pull it out and make sure you get thorough answers.

The first few days at home with your new Malamute puppy will probably be a combination of wonderful and frustrating. You may get a little less sleep than normal, but the bond you and your puppy are creating during the early days will be well worth the work you are putting in now, no matter how many messes you have to clean up along the way

CHAPTER 5
Being a Puppy Parent

Whether you've raised a puppy before or are a first time puppy parent, you will undoubtedly encounter unanticipated things. Every dog is different and comes with its own set of joys and troubles. This chapter will review many of the potential challenges you will encounter with your growing Malamute and help you navigate through them with minimal stress.

Photo Courtesy of Ana Maria Ciulcu.

Have Realistic Expectations

"With Malamute puppies you always need to expect the unexpected. Some love their special space or crate and some just want to be with their people. Some want their own bed and some want to sleep with you. Some will gobble their food and some will eat only when they feel like it."

Pat McGovern
ThunderKloud Alaskan Malamutes

The first thing you should remember before bringing your Malamute home is that it's not always easy or fun. Caring for a puppy is much like caring for a baby. It can be a demanding job that involves getting up in the middle of the night to take your dog outside, cleaning up accidents, and always keeping a watchful eye to be sure nothing is being destroyed by those sharp puppy teeth. No matter how well-mannered your puppy may seem, no puppy parents get by completely unscathed and many come away with at least a lost shoe or two.

If you think raising your new Malamute will be easy, you may want to reconsider. Puppies are challenging in general, but Malamutes are particularly independent and can pose an even greater challenge to train. The reward you will receive after going through the challenging phases together will be a well-mannered, properly trained, loyal, and loving Malamute.

Photo Courtesy of Nicky Adams

Chewing

One of the most frustrating things about caring for a puppy is the issue of chewing. Chewing is a way for puppies to explore the world and also relieve pain caused by incoming adult teeth. It is inevitable and unstoppable so don't reprimand your puppy for doing what comes naturally. Instead, be sure your puppy has plenty of safe toys or rubber bones to chew on so he's not tempted instead by your boot or the leg of the coffee table.

If you catch your puppy chewing on something inappropriate, remove the item or the puppy from the situation and give him an appropriate chew toy. This positive "take and replace" technique is much more effective than yelling at or punishing the puppy. Never let your puppy chew on your fingers or hands. It may be cute while he's little, but this is a habit that is very difficult to break once established.

If your puppy is a persistent chewer, you may want to invest in some bitter apple spray. This is intended to deter dogs from chewing due to its bad taste.

Chewing due to teething will most likely stop when all adult teeth have come in, around five to six months of age. However, some dogs chew more than others and will continue the habit into young adulthood. In these cases, it is important to always have a safe and desirable chew toy available to your Malamute.

Digging

Dogs dig for many reasons. Some dogs dig out of boredom, some because they're hot and want to lie in the cool dirt, and some just for the fun and adventure of it. The Alaskan Malamute is one breed that loves to dig! Notorious for leaving craters in the ground, Malamutes instinctively dig dens to keep warm in the winter and cool in the summer; something they had to do for survival in the Alaskan wilderness. Before bringing your Malamute home, you will need to take precautions around the yard to keep your plants, lawn, and dog safe.

If your Malamute is trying to dig under a fence, try to determine the reason he may be doing this. Is he not getting enough mental stimulation? Malamutes have high needs and will not do well alone, unoccupied. The curiosity of a bored Malamute can quickly lead him to seek out his own adventure under the fence.

Because digging comes so naturally to your Malamute, you may consider designating one area of your yard as a "digging zone." When you catch your Malamute digging in a no-dig zone, firmly correct him and take him im-

Photo Courtesy of Leah Porter

mediately to the digging zone. With enough training and persistence, you may be able to save your favorite bushes and avoid a yard full of holes.

If digging gets out of control, you may need to take a different approach. Try letting your Malamute outside under supervised conditions only. Allow your dog to do his business and then offer him a game of fetch. If you allow your Malamute to entertain himself, you may find craters in your yard. You will need to find other supervised ways to get your Malamute the exercise and stimulation he needs.

Running Away

Alaskan Malamutes are loyal dogs that loves their people. However, this won't stop your loving Malamute from seizing every opportunity for an adventure away. Given their curious and independent nature, Malamutes just can't seem to resist an opportunity to run away and see where their noses take them.

It is vital that you have secure fencing at least six feet tall to keep your Malamute in. Check it thoroughly for holes or any spaces where your dog could escape. If possible, sink your fence in the ground or set it in a base of concrete all around to prevent digging. If this is not possible, know that you will not be able to leave your Malamute unattended outside for long or he may not be there when you return.

An escaped Malamute can be a dangerous situation for other neighborhood animals, such as cats or rabbits. The prey drive is strong for a Malamute and can prove fatal for any small animals he encounters on his adventures away from home. Always make sure your Malamute wears a collar with ID tags and has a microchip so anyone who finds him can return him safely.

Photo Courtesy of
Ashley DePonceau

Howling, Barking, and Growling

A well-bred Malamute is naturally territorial with other animals, but generally quiet and friendly with people. Malamutes don't bark much, but they do love to "talk" to you in their endearing "woo woo" howl. When left alone too long, this endearing howl can become quite the nuisance and may need to be corrected. If you find howling has become a problem while you are away or at night, try distracting your Malamute with a rotation of new toys and chewables. Evaluate the cause of the problem, such as loneliness, and fix that or the problems may only continue to worsen.

If you're in the middle of a tug-of-war match with your puppy and hear him let out a vicious growl, you may be concerned. Take heart, though, because a puppy is usually not growling out of aggression. When puppies play, they will often display loud barking, growling, chasing, and pouncing. This is natural in a puppy's development and is exactly how they would be playing with their litter mates to establish new skills and better coordination.

If you want to discourage play fighting, don't do it by punishing your puppy. These are natural behaviors that should simply be ignored. If your puppy begins to play too rough and bark and growl, stop playing immediately and walk away. Come back to play when the puppy settles down. If your puppy continues to play too rough when you return, repeat the process until your puppy grasps the idea of what is and is not acceptable. This will take time but is well worth the effort.

If your dog seems truly agitated or begins nipping and biting in a way that seems defensive, it may be time to schedule a trip to see the vet. Truly agitated growling and biting behavior in a previously well-mannered dog can indicate a health problem that may be causing pain.

Separation Anxiety

"Alaskan Malamutes do not like being alone. If they do develop separation anxiety they can, and will, chew their way through your doors and walls. Exercise, exercise, exercise, and a strong crate are a must if they start to develop separation anxiety. To prevent it, don't leave them alone for long periods at first, then gradually work up to being gone for longer and longer times, making sure they always feel safe."

Brian Trujillo
Trujillo's Malamutes

Most puppies will whine or bark when left alone. This is normal behavior and will typically stop as the dog becomes accustomed to short spans of time alone. However, a dog with separation anxiety will bark and pace persistently until you return. He may become destructive, chewing and clawing things out of distress. Even a housetrained dog may urinate or defecate in the house repeatedly when left alone if he suffers from separation anxiety. In extreme cases, a dog may display signs of coprophagy, a condition when a dog defecates and then consumes the stool.

Separation anxiety can occur in any dog. Treating separation anxiety takes patience and understanding. Dogs, especially Malamutes, are pack animals and instinctually do not like to be alone. The anxiety they feel stems from a very real and primal fear of being abandoned.

It may be helpful to take your dog for a jog or play an exhaustive game of fetch with him just before you leave. Hopefully, this will tire your dog out and he will be too exhausted to get worked up while you're gone. You can also try leaving your dog with an interactive toy. Try a treat ball or a dog puzzle that will reward him with treats periodically. This may be just enough distraction to get your dog through his time alone. Make this toy or puzzle a special thing your Malamute only gets when he's alone. This can help positively reinforce that being alone can be a treat.

If the separation anxiety is severe and nothing seems to work, make an appointment with your vet to check that there is nothing else going on. They may be able to advise you on some safe ways to keep your dog calm when you have to leave the house.

While Malamutes are not particularly prone to true separation anxiety, they may still become destructive if they are left alone for too long. Malamutes are very good at finding things to occupy them while they are alone, even if that means spending an hour ripping every stitch of stuffing out of your couch cushion or shredding the blinds.

Crate Training Basics

"Crate training is a must. You don't want to just bring home the puppy and turn them loose to run all over the house. That is only setting yourself up for disaster! Potty training is so much easier and you will far fewer accidents."

Loretta Roach
Mountain Ridge Malamutes

Photo Courtesy of
Katy Rozman

Crate training is a controversial topic among dog owners. Some believe the crate is a cage and inhumane. Others believe the crate is a necessary tool used to protect and secure a dog. The fact is, when done properly, crating your dog is an excellent tool for housetraining and will set your dog up for success from the start.

When shopping for a crate, there are multiple types to choose from. These include plastic crates, wire crates, soft crates, and heavy-duty crates. The two main types are plastic and wire. If you plan to travel with your dog by plane, you will need to purchase a plastic crate as these are the only crates allowed for air travel.

Another common type of crate is the wire crate. These crates allow more visibility and airflow. They also fold flat for easy storage when not in use. These crates, depending on the size, often come with a removable divider. This is an excellent tool to use when potty training your new puppy as it keeps the space small, so your puppy doesn't soil one end. You can line your crate with a commercial crate pad or an old towel or blanket for comfort. Regardless of what type of crate you buy, be sure you get one big enough for your Malamute when he is fully grown or else you may end up having to buy another one.

The key to crate training is positive reinforcement. The crate is intended to be a safe haven for your dog, a place he can go for rest and comfort. Do not ever put your dog in the crate as a form of punishment. This sends the message that the crate is a bad place and will create issues going forward. You don't want your dog to view the crate as a "timeout" box or he will never retreat there willingly.

The first time you introduce your new puppy to the crate, you'll want to have some training treats on hand. Secure the door of the crate to the side so it doesn't accidentally swing closed and scare your puppy. Begin by placing a treat or two outside, near the door of the crate. Depending on how your Malamute reacts to the crate, slowly place the treats closer until you can put one inside. Your puppy should voluntarily go inside the crate to get it.

Don't shut the door of the crate the first few times he goes in. Instead, praise him and allow him to come in and out of the crate freely. After your puppy becomes comfortable with the open crate, guide him in there and gently latch the door. Give him treats from the outside crate and verbally praise him. This will help him feel comfortable. Practice this exercise the first day you get your puppy home to get him fully comfortable with the crate before his first night in it.

Any time you need to crate your dog, do so by rewarding him with treats and a special toy. Praise him and make it a fun experience to get inside the crate. Don't leave your dog in the crate for long the first few times, with the exception of nighttime, or he may begin to get anxious and associate those feelings with the crate. Practice leaving your puppy in the crate while you're home for short increments of time, thirty minutes to an hour. Always immediately take your dog outside to his potty area when you let him out of the crate.

Photo Courtesy of Megan Sharman

Be sure to exercise your Malamute thoroughly before expecting him to have any crate time. It is not reasonable to put your dog in a crate without first allowing him to expend his energy. Doing this will allow him to rest and sleep in his crate while you're away, further minimizing the chances of destruction or separation anxiety. Bored Malamutes can do seemingly impossible things and have been known to force their way from a kennel, gaining free range of the house while their owners are away. Avoid these problems by giving your Malamute vigorous exercise beforehand and ensure that you provide toys to occupy him while he is alone in the crate.

The crate is a tool that should be used responsibly. Never leave your dog in a crate for an extended period of time or treat the crate like a dog sitter. Hopefully, with proper training, your puppy will outgrow his need for the crate and will no longer need to be confined to it while you're sleeping or away. Until then, always use the crate with care. If your puppy doesn't view the crate as a place of rest and comfort, you may need to reevaluate the way you're using it.

When you return from your first trip away, it may seem fitting to greet your puppy with an excited hello, but refrain so you don't make your dog think getting out of the crate is more exciting than going in. Going in the crate should be fun and exciting but getting out should be no big deal. Open the door to the crate casually and without much fuss. Remember, the crate is a safe and secure place of rest for your Malamute, not a place of punishment. If you let your dog out of the crate with too much excitement, you will inadvertently train him to be hyper and overexcited when the crate door opens.

Crate training will take time and effort. Some dogs take to it quickly and easily while others need more time and practice. When dealing with an Alaskan Malamute, training can be challenging. It is important to find solutions that work for both you and your dog. Establish yourself as the leader of the pack but be considerate of your Malamute's needs and wants as well.

CHAPTER 6
Alaskan Malamutes and Your Other Pets

Introducing Your Malamute to Other Animals

"Introduce them with a gate between them initially so they can see and smell their new friend and get used to them. After they settle down, they can be introduced on lead and eventually off lead. NEVER introduce adults unless both are calm and under control."

Pat McGovern
ThunderKloud Alaskan Malamutes

Photo Courtesy of Sarah Schmidt

Alaskan Malamutes possess a strong prey drive that can make it dangerous to introduce them to other pets. It's best to keep small animals like birds, rodents, and rabbits away from your Malamute if they don't need to interact. If you have a pet of another species that you want to interact

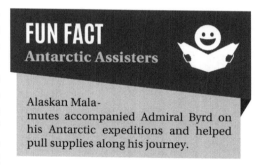

FUN FACT
Antarctic Assisters

Alaskan Malamutes accompanied Admiral Byrd on his Antarctic expeditions and helped pull supplies along his journey.

with your Malamute, begin the introductions as young as possible and with constant supervision.

To introduce your new Malamute puppy to a resident cat, begin by exchanging the animals' scents. Keeping the animals separated, place a blanket or toy with the puppy's scent near the cat. Do the same for the puppy in a different area of the house. Let the dog and the cat sniff and become accustomed to the scents before a face-to-face interaction.

After exchanging scents, allow your pets to indirectly interact. Keep them separated by a gate or the crate but allow them to view each other. Depending on their reactions, you may feel comfortable enough to let them loose but be careful – if your Malamute puppy is very young, he probably can't do much damage to your cat, but your cat can definitely harm your puppy if he feels threatened. Try introductions with someone gently holding each animal. Let the two sniff and explore but watch carefully for claws. Praise both animals for calm and reasonable reactions. Stop the introduction immediately if there is any fear or aggression shown.

Most likely, a very young Malamute pup will just want to make friends with your cat, but for a slightly older Malamute puppy, the introduction may not be as easy. An Alaskan Malamute pup will grow quickly, making it easier for your pup to harm your other animals. If your Malamute is having a difficult time coexisting with cat, take things slowly and never leave them unsupervised. Make sure your cat can always escape. This escape should be off the ground in an area where your dog can't reach.

The best way to introduce a Malamute into your family with other dogs is to do it when the animals are very young. Practice the same guidelines as when introducing a Malamute puppy to a cat. Even if your Malamute puppy seems to fit into the family with ease, always remain aware of potential issues down the road as your dog matures. If your Malamute is triggered by something, fights between these dogs can be brutal and dangerous.

Introducing an Older Dog

HELPFUL TIP

Proper Socialization is Crucial

Alaskan Malamutes can learn to behave around cats and other small animals, but they have an instinctive urge to hunt that can cause problems if they aren't well-socialized. If you have cats, you may be better off getting a puppy rather than trying to introduce an adult Malamute into the family.

You will need to take a different approach to introducing an adult Malamute to a resident cat. An adult Malamute can cause real harm to a cat and the cat can do the same. Begin with the scent exchange described above.

After a day of permitting the animals to become accustomed to the other's scent, allow the two to meet through a closed door. Depending on personality, neither pet may be very interested in the other or they may be busting down the door to see who is on the other side. Allow each animal to become calm and relaxed before any face-to-face interactions.

Once the two have become relaxed and calm on both sides of the door, allow them to meet with the dog on a loose leash. Be sure to keep a firm grip on the leash and have a helper who is capable of holding your dog back in the event your Malamute tries to chase the cat. Allow the animals a brief interaction before separating them and distracting them to divert their attention. If the initial interaction was calm and peaceful, try again. If you decide to let the two interact with your dog off-leash, always allow your cat to escape to his safe space, designated just for him. Remember the Malamute's strong prey drive and handle these face-to-face interactions with extreme caution.

Introducing your older Malamute to another dog can be just as challenging. Malamutes can be territorial and will compete to be the alpha amongst themselves, especially when it involves dogs of the same sex.

The reality for a Malamute is he may not ever exist peacefully with other animals in your home. The dominance and the prey drive is just too strong for some. Introducing your Malamute as a very young puppy can make these interspecies relationships possible but you will still need to be careful and always keep a watchful eye.

The Pack Mentality

"Malamutes are a pack dog and they look at each member of the family as part of their pack. Pack order is established during the bonding stage of introduction to the family, and each member should be included in that process."

Gail Partain
Windwalker Malamutes

Photo Courtesy of
Sandra Zetschok

Photo Courtesy of Kayla Shupe

Wolves and dogs in the wild have strict social orders they follow. This is the "pack mentality." In every wild pack there is an Alpha male and an Alpha female. These are the two pack leaders. At the bottom of the pack is the Omega. Other animals in the pack fall somewhere between the Alpha and Omega.

The struggle for survival in the Alaskan wilderness has allowed Alaskan Malamutes to remain instinctively pack-minded dogs. This is why it can be so challenging for your Malamute to coexist with other dogs. Packs in the wild follow strict social rules and anyone who steps out of line will face the consequences. When a member of the pack challenges the alpha, he is intending to take the alpha's place as pack leader. Fights among the pack during times of stress or challenge can be brutal when there is a power struggle and can leave one or more dogs seriously injured or dead. A healthy, functioning pack, where all dogs have established their place, will still fight, but injuries should be minimal.

When raising a Malamute, it is critical to establish yourself as alpha as early as possible. Be firm with corrections and let your Malamute know you are the one in charge. If you can successfully establish yourself as the pack leader, you may minimize alpha aggression later down the road. At any point your Malamute tries to challenge your leadership position, quickly and firmly correct his behavior so he will know you are still in charge.

Bad Behavior – How to Correct It

The Alaskan Malamute can be a challenging breed to raise and live with. If your Malamute does display aggressive behaviors, first take your dog to the vet to be sure there is no underlying condition causing him pain. Once this is ruled out it's time to evaluate the dog's current situation. Is there anything causing your Malamute unnecessary stress? Is he being left alone too long? Is he being given enough attention and exercise? Is your Malamute clashing with other animals in your home?

If your Malamute is showing aggression toward other dogs, begin by taking the proper steps to socialize him. Because of the Malamute's brute strength and natural aggression toward other animals, it is recommended this socialization training is done by a professional. Take it slowly and don't progress to direct interactions until your dog can keep his cool consistently. For dogs dealing with aggression issues, this could take much longer to achieve.

If your dog is showing aggression toward other pets at home, first begin by identifying the source. Is it food aggression? Does your Malamute become possessive over toys or treats? Malamutes are especially prone to being food aggressive because of their survivalist history in Alaska. When food was scarce, protecting what they had was a matter of life or death.

If you identify the source of aggression, remove it. If your dog is dealing with food aggression, eliminate the situation by feeding your Malamute in another room, away from all other pets. If he is particularly possessive of a favorite toy, only allow him to have the toy in the confines of his crate or designated alone area. Removing your dog from the stressful situations will not solve the aggression problem, but it will make life easier while you deal with the root cause.

An aggressive Malamute can be dangerous and unpredictable, especially if his past is unknown. Malamutes are independent and stubborn, and their size can make them hard to handle when dealing with aggression. Only you can judge the severity of the situation. If the aggression doesn't improve or evolves to physical harm in any way, seek a professional trainer's help immediately. Never leave a potentially aggressive dog alone with another animal, child, or unfamiliar person.

Rough Play or Aggression?

Many dogs growl and bare their teeth when they play. This does not automatically mean your dog has aggression issues. In fact, sometimes it can be quite difficult to distinguish between play and aggression.

When your dog and another dog are playfully bowing and taking turns chasing, rolling over, and mouthing each other, these are all signs that they are engaging in play together. Allowing this play to continue offers your dog great practice with social skills and is a wonderful outlet for excess energy.

If the dogs are playing but one or both seem stiff and tense, there may be more than a playful romp going on between them. Deep, drawn out growling, staring into the other dog's eyes, and a one-sided chase may all be

Photo Courtesy of Jennifer Norwood

indications that one or both of the dogs are showing some real aggression and you may want to end the encounter.

If you're having trouble with your puppy or adult dog playing too rough with you, the best thing to do is ignore him. In a pack, older dogs will naturally teach the younger pups when enough is enough. They do this by using verbal cues and then ending play immediately. Even puppies of the same litter do this to each other. As the owner, you can take the same stance to establish yourself as alpha. When play becomes too rough, yip loudly and then walk away, ignoring your dog. After a minute, once the dog seems to have shifted his attention, return to play. Repeat this process until the puppy understands the rough play is not acceptable. Eventually he will understand the reason you keep walking away and will lessen his intensity.

Be aware of how you approach your dog for play. If you come in swinging and throwing your hands and arms around, this is encouraging your dog to play rough. Use toys instead of your body and keep movements gentle.

How to Break Up a Dog Fight

When a fight does break out, it can be intimidating trying to stop it. Jumping in the middle of two large dogs can lead to serious injury, even if neither dog intends to direct their aggression toward you. Here are a few helpful tips to successfully stop a dog fight and regain control of the situation.

Use Loud Noises

The method of operation in this strategy is distraction. Find something close that makes a loud, disruptive noise. This may be an airhorn or even a wooden spoon banging on a metal pot. If you can successfully distract the dogs and get their eyes off of one another, use that opportunity to cover the dog's heads with blankets and separate them.

Spray Them with Water

If your dogs are fighting outside, grab the water hose and hose them both down. This will distract them long enough to hopefully end the aggression. This also allows you to keep a safe distance while further establishing yourself as pack leader, disapproving of the aggressive behavior.

Wheelbarrow Method

If you are with someone capable of helping you diffuse the situation, you may use the "wheelbarrow method" to separate the dogs. Each of you should carefully get behind a dog and grab its back legs, pulling the dog away from the other backwards. Malamutes are strong and determined so only attempt this method if you are certain you will be able to manage the dog.

Use good judgement and only approach aggressive dogs with extreme caution. Your dog may mean no harm toward you, but you may still get caught in the crosshairs of the tussle. If your Malamute is consistently becoming aggressive with other animals in your home, you need to seek professional help right away. Do not let aggressive behavior continue or it will only get worse for your Malamute.

What Happens if My Pets Don't Get Along?

"My Malamute puppies are usually scared of toy dog breeds. Little dogs with big attitudes are intimidating so watch to make sure the little dogs don't bite them. Also, don't let a cat scratch them or they will remember that pain and associate pain with cats."

Randy Checketts
Chex Alaskan Malamutes

One of the most frustrating things about owning an Alaskan Malamute is their common inability to get along with other dogs. Before you bring an Alaskan Malamute into your home with other animals, consider the consequences if he does not mesh well. Will you be able to give him the training and time he needs to help diffuse the situation? What will happen if you cannot diffuse the situation?

Considering all of these possibilities before committing to an Alaskan Malamute is important. Malamutes are often recommended for homes where there are no other dogs or animals. You do not want to bring a dog home only to realize you have to rehome him because you did not do your due diligence. This is the sad reality for many Malamutes in rescue centers today.

CHAPTER 7
Socializing Your New Malamute

Importance of Socialization

"As soon as they have had their first and second set of shots start taking them to places that allows pets. Socializing is extremely important in a pups first four months of life."

Loretta Roach
Mountain Ridge Malamutes

M alamute puppies have a critical age between 8-16 weeks in which they are highly impressionable. They will soak up everything like a sponge, and what they experience during this time will lay the foundation for how they react to things as they grow older. Malamutes are naturally social toward humans, showing love and affection to friends and strangers alike. However, without early and proper socialization, your Malamute will potentially struggle to live harmoniously with dogs or other animals. By beginning your dog's socialization early, you can do your best to help him co-exist with any people or dogs he encounters in any environment. This will make life easier for you if you take your dog for walks at the park, restaurants, or other crowded outdoor events.

Photo Courtesy of Tom O'Hennessy

Behavior Around Other Dogs

"If your Malamute displays aggression towards another animal, correct the behavior by making a game of it: down play the aggression, but get the dog or puppies attention, so that it doesn't escalate into a fight. Take him or her away from the other animal and then try it again, rewarding for good behavior."

Gail Partain

Windwalker Malamutes

Imagine a world where people greeted each other the way dogs do by sniffing, circling, and jumping up and down playfully. That would be quite a silly sight! Luckily for us, we humans have strict social guidelines to follow when we encounter each other. Dogs also have a set of social rules, but they are not nearly as strict as ours.

Much like people, dogs greet each other differently at a first meeting than they greet an old friend and much of it depends on the individual dog's personality. Dogs typically greet each other in one or all of the following ways:

Sniffing: Probably the most notable and joked about canine ritual is the sniff test. When dogs greet one another, they may begin with the muzzle or go straight for the backside. Sometimes the sniff will be brief and sometimes it can seem like a full blown investigation. Unless one dog seems uncomfortable, this is perfectly normal behavior and doesn't need to be stopped. Once the dogs have satisfied their sniffers, they can move on to the next step in the canine greeting.

Play Stance: Have you ever seen a dog approach another dog and immediately go into a play bow? This behavior is simply one dog attempting to initiate play. It's like he's saying "Hey there! Do you want to be friends

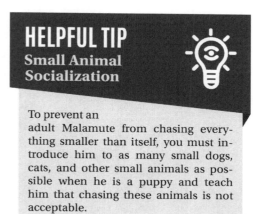

HELPFUL TIP
Small Animal Socialization

To prevent an adult Malamute from chasing everything smaller than itself, you must introduce him to as many small dogs, cats, and other small animals as possible when he is a puppy and teach him that chasing these animals is not acceptable.

85

and play together?" Even a quick playful growl accompanied by a friendly tail wag is acceptable. Again, as long as neither dog seems stressed, there is no need to stop this behavior. Even if the other dog declines the offer to play, that doesn't mean the meeting was not successful.

Exerting Dominance: This particular greeting is probably the least endearing to a human onlooker, but is still acceptable in the canine world. One dog may exert his dominance by being the first to sniff and by non-aggressively showing the other dog he is in charge. This could include mounting. This process may be obvious to you or it may all happen so quickly that you don't even notice until little Sparky rolls over to show his belly in submission. As with the other behaviors, these are the natural social ways of dogs and should not be stopped unless there is real aggression or stress. Dogs take social cues well and are pretty good at keeping each other in line. If one is displeased, he will probably let other dogs know pretty quickly.

Photo Courtesy of Sarah Schmidt

Photo Courtesy of Daniel and Karina Wheater

Safe Ways to Socialize

The way dogs behave around each other can vary from breed to breed and dog to dog. If you're bringing your Malamute home as a puppy, socializing him with other dogs as early as possible is mandatory to prevent issues with aggression in his future. In general, puppies are more adaptable and willing to meet other dogs. Socialization should begin as early as possible, but be sure not to allow your puppy to have close contact with dogs you don't know until he has had his complete series of puppy shots.

If you choose to socialize your puppy with a leash on, keep your puppy close on leash or on the other side of a barrier, such as a gate, when you make introductions with other dogs, especially those that are older or larger. Preferably all other dogs should also be leashed or somehow restrained in case anything goes wrong.

Allow the dogs to greet each other for a few seconds and then walk away. Each owner should distract their dog at this point until they are no longer interested in the other dog. If the initial interaction went well, allow the dogs to come together again in the same manner. Keep the leash loose so the dog can maneuver but not so loose it becomes a tangled mess. Read each dog's body language to determine how the greeting is going. Bodies should be relaxed and there should be no staring contests. As the dogs become comfortable and relaxed with each other, you will be able to let them off leash and they can have supervised play.

Some trainers believe first time dog greetings should always be done off leash so that the dogs are allowed to behave and greet each other more

naturally. They believe that some dogs will feel trapped by the leash and become more defensive in nature, making the greeting unnatural and awkward. If this is the method you choose, make sure the owners of both dogs are fully compliant and willing to meet in a safe and neutral fenced area.

A first time greeting should never be done in one of the dogs' yards. This could be seen as an invasion of territory for some dogs and cause a defensive reaction. Allow the dogs to meet but monitor their body language. If they use the body language described above, you don't need to interfere. But if either dog seems stiff, uncomfortable, or agitated, separate the dogs and use distractions to get their attention off of each other. Off leash greetings can bring a greater risk if you don't know the other dog well and should only be done with friendly, pre-socialized dogs. Safety is the most important thing when socializing your dog so only do what you feel comfortable with.

Socializing Adult Dogs

If you're bringing an adult Malamute into your home, the socialization process may take some extra time and careful planning. Depending on the dog's previous situation, he may not be used to other dogs. Oftentimes with a rescue, you don't know exactly what his life has held up until the point he was rescued. He may have been kept in a cage his whole life, abused by his owner, or may even been previously attacked by another dog. All of these things are unknowns that could have a significant impact on a Malamute's social abilities.

Be patient with your dog, no matter his age, and allow him to socialize on his terms. If your dog seems to have trouble socializing, take it slow and avoid putting your dog in situations that will cause him stress. This will only cause setbacks. Some dogs simply do best in one-dog households and shouldn't be pushed to live in uncomfortable circumstances for them (and everyone else!).

When dealing with an unsocialized adult Malamute, begin slowly at home. Take your dog on a walk around your neighborhood where he can see other dogs indirectly. He should eventually become comfortable enough to walk by other dogs in their backyards or on leashes without becoming stressed. When he has successfully mastered these indirect encounters, it's time to move on to the next step.

If you have a neighbor with a dog, this is a great place to start direct socialization. These dogs will probably encounter each other at one point or another and will benefit by getting to know each other. Ask your neighbor and arrange a time to allow both dogs to meet, on leash, in a neutral part of the yard. Take things slow and give them space if either seems stressed. Follow the three second rule and then walk away and distract each dog. Allow the dogs to come together again if the first encounter went well. If it doesn't seem to be going well, that's okay! Allow the dogs to just be in the yard at the same time until they become used to each other and then gradually allow them to interact more as it seems appropriate.

Keep your demeanor calm and stress free so that your dog doesn't pick up on any tension. It's all about establishing trust between you and your dog and between your dog and your neighbor's dog. Speak to your neighbor and his dog in a friendly and confident tone to help show your Malamute they're not a threat.

Dog Parks

"Start early and socialize them often. Take them to puppy play groups, sign them up for puppy classes, and be careful of dog parks. A negative experience in an uncontrolled environment like the dog park can have the opposite effect."

Brian Trujillo
Trujillo's Malamutes

If you don't have a neighboring dog, call a friend with a dog or take your dog to a dog park. A dog park can be overwhelming depending on how many dogs are there so this may be a last resort as a place to socialize. Begin by just walking around the perimeter at a comfortable distance. Listen to your dog and take his cues. If he seems comfortable, allow him to interact more closely with a dog through the fence. If he remains calm, praise him. Reward him for positive encounters and remove him from negative ones. Try to only let him interact with dogs that are also calm. It will not help the situation to engage with a loud, barking, rambunctious dog through the fence. This could cause stress for an unsocialized dog and stop progress.

Dog Parks can be a good way to socialize your Malamute, but even so, be cautious. These parks can be a breeding ground for diseases and are not suitable for young puppies. This can also quickly become an uncontrollable, aggressive environment, especially when introducing an unsocial Alaskan Malamute. Do not put your own dog or the other dogs at risk by allowing your Malamute too much freedom at the dog park.

Another great option for socializing your Malamute with other dogs is to enroll in a beginning obedience class at a local training center. This should only be done after your pup has had his full series of puppy shots. Arrive at least 10-15 minutes before the class begins and sit quietly with your dog (on his leash), so that he can get accustomed to the environment. Once the class begins, he will be focused on learning the basics of obedience while surrounded by other dogs. You will also learn how to teach him valuable commands like heel, sit, stay, and come.

Meeting New People

Introducing a Malamute puppy to new people should be easy. Remember, puppies are generally easygoing and make new friends well. This is especially true for a Malamute pup. The main thing you will want to teach your puppy about meeting new people is not to jump. This can be challenging because when your puppy is small the jumping may seem cute. However, once the dog grows, the jumping becomes a problem and it's much harder to correct the behavior if it was once allowed. Remember, a Malamute needs strong rules enforced early in order to keep yourself in the alpha position as he matures. Any confusion about who is in charge can lead to a rebellious Malamute as he matures.

Ideally, when approached by a person, your puppy should have a minimal reaction. He should remain calm but happy and keep all four paws on the ground. If you need to stop a jumping habit, begin by teaching your dog an alternate command. "Sit" is a good command to combat jumping be-

Photo Courtesy of
Adam Monument

cause your dog can't do both at the same time. When your dog gets over-ly excited and begins to jump, counter by giving the "sit" command. Reward him for sitting and staying calm. If he can't stay calm and continues to jump, leave the room and ignore your dog for thirty seconds to one minute. Return and try again. This process works well for meeting new people, getting the leash out for walks, or any other exciting event that gets your dog jumping.

Introducing a rescue dog to new people can be a different story. Not knowing your Malamute's past means not knowing if he's had any negative human interactions. Begin any new introductions with people much like you would with dogs, slow and controlled. If your rescue Malamute is a bit socially stunted, you probably had to work to gain his trust. Apply those same principles to anyone you want to introduce to your dog.

If you're having guests over, ask those people ahead of time to remain calm and not show the dog much attention. This may help ease your Malamute's mind and keep him calm. If your guests want to rub and love all over him, even with the best intentions, it could cause him to become over-excited and stressed. Once calm and comfortable, the dog may be trusting enough to allow a belly rub or two, but it should always be on his own terms. Give your guests some training treats to gain the dog's trust. If your dog is particularly shy and nervous and you don't see much progress being made, try separating him with a baby gate so that he can observe people but not feel pressured or overwhelmed.

Don't be afraid to take your Malamute into other situations where he can meet people. One of the best places for this is in your local big box home improvement store. Most of them not only allow dogs but welcome them warmly. It's hard to make your way from the electrical department to the lumber area without a dozen or so friendly people asking to pet your Malamute! Have a few small treats handy and ask people to give one to your dog – he will quickly learn that meeting people is a good experience.

With enough patience and diligence, most Malamutes can become well socialized with people. A well-bred Malamute should make the process easier, but it's still important to follow the guidelines above for the safety of your own dog and others. If your Malamute is aggressive toward people, do not socialize him in a public place where there are unsuspecting adults and children. You may think nothing bad can happen, but an unpredictable Malamute can cause serious harm to anyone due to his strength and size, and if he is triggered into aggression, you may not be able to stop him.

Alaskan Malamutes and Children

Malamutes, despite their aggressive tendencies toward other animals, are known for being excellent with children. They are patient and loving, often creating strong bonds with the young ones in the house. Their sheer size and strength can make it possible for your loving Malamute to cause them unintentional harm, however, so it is still important to keep cautious boundaries with small children.

Always teach your children to be gentle and kind, never pulling his ears, hair, or tail. Show them by example the proper way to pet and hold your Malamute puppy so that they understand how to safely handle him. No matter how friendly and trustworthy your Malamute is, never leave a child and dog alone unattended. This is for the safety of both the child and the dog.

CHAPTER 8
Physical and Mental Exercise

Exercise Requirements

"All Malamutes are different and each will need their own amount of exercise. It's all in the individual dog. You never want to exercise them to much as pups as their joints are still growing and fusing together. An excessive amount of exercise as a baby can cause long term joint issues later in their lives."

Christy Nash
Oregon Malamutes

All dog breeds need regular exercise to keep them in good shape. That said, Malamutes need more. Bred to work, these dogs do best when they are given a purpose and a job to accomplish. Without it, Malamutes become bored and destructive and often are deemed out of control. This trait is no fault, it is a drive still intact from their days surviving in the Alaskan wilderness with the Inuit people.

How to Make Exercise Fun

"If at all possible take your Malamute for a walk in the morning and the evening. Weight pulling is also a good exercise for them, we all know Malamutes love to pull and they really enjoy it. Teaching them to play fetch is a great source of exercise too."

Loretta Roach
Mountain Ridge Malamutes

If you don't live in an area where sled pulling is an option, there are other ways to make exercising your dog fun and exciting. Sometimes walking or jogging the same block or route in the park can become mundane, but walking your Malamute is not the only way to get your dog's heart pumping. Try some of the following ideas to help you and your dog get past an exercise slump.

Use a Flirt Pole – A flirt pole is basically a stick with a toy attached to the end with a string. It allows you to engage your dog in a game of chase without much movement of your own. You can even use the flirt pole from a seated position. Because of a Malamute's natural prey drive, a flirt pole is a great option for some low impact activity for you and your dog. The flirt pole engages your dog mentally and physically, a win-win!

Play Hide and Seek – Once your dog has mastered basic commands and can sit and stay, try engaging him in a game of hide and seek. Take your dog to a chosen location in the house and have him sit and stay where he is. Your job is to go hide elsewhere in the house and then call him when you are ready.

If your dog won't stay still long enough to allow you to hide, try giving him a treat that will take him half a minute or so to finish. Once he finishes, call to him from your hiding place and see how long it takes him to find you. Keep giving him encouragement until he figures out where you are. The game is fun for you and him alike and is a great way to give him a little exercise on a rainy day.

Play Fetch – So simple, yet so effective! There is not much a dog loves more than a game of fetch. Play with a tennis ball, rope, or Frisbee. Mix it up to keep things interesting. Teach your dog to return the item to your lap and this game can be a consistently easy outlet for excess energy.

Scavenger Hunt – A typical dog has up to 300 million olfactory receptors in his nose and the part of a dog's brain devoted to smell is proportionally 40 times larger than a human's. That means your Alaskan Malamute has a powerful sniffer! Make mealtime or snack time fun by creating a game out of it and putting that nose to work.

Hide small amounts of food or treats around areas of a room and see if your dog can sniff them out. If you hide treats in enough areas, your Malamute may find himself running around the room from spot to spot trying to find the sources of the smell. While this may not provide as much exercise as one of the previous suggestions, it is still a way to get a lazy dog motivated on a dreary day.

Dog Daycare – Even if you spend most of your time home with your dog, an occasional trip to a local dog day care is a great way to give your pup some play time with other dogs while also allowing you to run errands without leaving your Malamute alone. After a few hours at day care, your Malamute will probably be exhausted and ready for a relaxing nap at home. This is only an option for a well socialized Malamute that gets along well with other dogs.

Photo Courtesy of Sara Maida

Importance of Mental Exercise

Although physical exercise usually gets all the attention, mental stimulation for your Malamute is equally as important. Your Malamute is both highly intelligent and determined and needs to have an outlet for all of that brain power. These traits were put to good use as working dogs, but as house pets, they need something else to fill the gaps.

Tips for Keeping Your Malamute Occupied

"A tired Malamute is a happy Malamute."

Pat McGovern
ThunderKloud Alaskan Malamutes

Photo Courtesy of Elizabeth Hendrix

Many of the suggestions above serve as mental exercise as well as physical. Playing hide and seek, doing scavenger hunts, and using a flirt pole all provide a high amount of direct mental stimulation, as does interacting with other dogs at dog daycare.

Another way to mentally stimulate your Malamute is by teaching him a new trick. Malamutes love to please – as long as it pleases them, to – and will enjoy a challenging training session. Learning a new command will help to further build the relationship and trust between you two, resulting in a generally more obedient and willing dog. After he has mastered all of the basic commands, get creative and teach your Malamute some fun tricks like jumping through a hoop, walking backward, or crawling. You can

Photo Courtesy of Chelsea Murray

even teach him to retrieve his toys by name and put them back up in their designated places. These are excellent tools for keeping your Malamute happy and content as a house dog.

There are toys and puzzles designed specifically with mental stimulation in mind. Kong makes a range of toys that can keep your dog occupied for a long time and are basically indestructible. A favorite is the "Classic Dog Toy." This is a rubber toy with a hollow center made for stuffing with treats. Kong has a safe line of treats and snacks or you can simply fill the toy with peanut butter. The Kong is dishwasher safe and costs between $8 and $25, depending on size, making it a great, affordable option.

Another option is a dog puzzle. The Trixie Poker Box has four compartments all covered by a lid. Your dog must figure out how each lid can be removed to get the reward waiting inside. All four lids open differently so this will take some real focus and determination on your dog's part. Once your dog figures out the trick to opening all boxes, this puzzle may not present a challenge anymore and he may want to move onto something else, so keep it in your arsenal for when your dog must be left alone.

If you prefer a mentally stimulating toy without the use of treats, try getting your Malamute an Outward Hound Hide A Squirrel Puzzle Dog Toy. It's a hollow, plush tree stump with holes around it. Inside there are three plush squirrels that squeak. Your dog will have tons of fun trying to pull the squirrels from the stump. This is a great option for a dog who may need to watch his weight but probably won't last long in the mouth of a Malamute as the squirrels are plush and can be torn apart with enough effort.

There are also electronic devices that you can control from a mobile device. Clever Pet is a unique system that challenges your dog with sequences, memory games, and electronically released treats or food when solved. This system comes with a light up pad that shows different colors and patterns. Clever Pet is designed to progressively get more challenging as your dog figures it out. Use the mobile application to track progress and monitor use. This system is wonderful for dogs who are left alone for long periods of the day. It comes at a $250 price tag, but is worth it if it means you don't have to spend money cleaning up after a bored, destructive Malamute.

If your dog loves a game of fetch, check out the iFetch Frenzy. Not as high-tech as the original iFetch, which is electronic and can launch a tennis ball up to 30 feet, the iFetch Frenzy uses gravity instead of electricity to drop the ball through one of three holes and send it rolling across the floor. As long as your Malamute can learn to return the ball to the top, he can play solo fetch for hours while you are away.

If you find that your Malamute has become particularly adept at performing tricks, you might want to look into earning him a title as a Trick Dog. The AKC awards Novice, Intermediate, and Advanced Trick Dog titles. You will need to teach your Malamute ten tricks from a prescribed list, and then go to a show where a judge will evaluate your dog's performance. If successful, you and your dog will both be rewarded for doing what is already a fun activity.

When you have to leave your Malamute alone for a time, rotate interactive toys that will help to keep him entertained while you are away. Some owners even like to leave the television on while they're gone. There are specific shows on DogTV that are geared specifically toward dogs that some pooches really seem to enjoy!

Photo Courtesy of
Leah Porter

Dog Sports and Activities

If you live in an area where snow is plentiful, there are many opportunities for you to get back to your dog's roots by engaging in some of the breed's original activities. Below is a list of sports and activities you and your Malamute can do together whether you live in a winter climate or a warm one.

Sledding or Mushing

While racing is not a Malamute's strong suit, they are built for force, strength and endurance. If you live in a winter climate, check local Malamute breeders for information on any sled strength competitions. Not only will your Malamute thrive in this environment, your relationship with your dog will flourish when you are working together for a purpose.

Photo Courtesy of
Chelsea Murray

If you have no experience with dog sledding, it is recommended that you seek professional help or seek out experienced mushers for help and advice. Check around with local breeders for sledding clubs nearby or go to sledddogcentral.com for a list of clubs based by region. Sledding can be extremely dangerous for you and your Malamute if not done properly.

If you decide to train your dog to pull a sled, there are four main supplies you will need:

- Pulling harness
- Tow rope
- Waist belt
- Sled or cart

When considering training your dog to pull a sled, you may want to find a local who is willing to lend you a pulling harness until you know whether or not you and your dog enjoy the sport. Pulling harnesses can be pricey and you will probably need an expert's opinion, either a seller or a local musher, to help you decide which is best for your Malamute.

Basic Sledding Commands

Lineout: Gets your dog in the ready position, standing up with some tension on the line

Hike: Start moving forward
On By: Instructs your pup to ignore an object or person and move on by
Gee: Turn right
Haw: Turn left
Easy: Slow down
Whoa: Stop

Basic Beginner Training Method

After your dog has been professionally fitted for a harness, attach the tow rope to your Malamute and to yourself via your waist belt. Begin your training by introducing him to the basic sledding commands while pulling you, slowly and in a straight line. This basic training will take weeks of hard work to accomplish.

As your dog becomes accustomed to pulling you and to responding to his new set of commands, you will be able to add more complicated elements, such as turns. With proper training, your dog will be able to pull the weight of a sled in due time.

HELPFUL TIP
Not for Couch Potatoes

Since Alaskan Malamutes were bred to work all day long, they have a lot of energy and require plenty of exercise. This breed is not well-suited for apartment life, and if you work away from home all day, then a dog walker or doggie day care can help keep a bored Malamute out of trouble.

Skijoring

An alternative to mushing, skijoring is a sport in which a cross country skier is pulled by anywhere from 1 to 3 dogs. The skier uses his skis and poles as well as the strength of his dogs on harnesses. The less common summer alternative to this sport is roller-skijoring.

Both sledding and skijoring are potentially dangerous sports if you and your dog do not follow proper training. As mentioned before, contacting local Malamute breeders should offer you many resources for local dog sports groups and trainers. If you are up to the challenge, both of these winter pulling sports are a perfect way for you and your dog to challenge each other and grow as companions.

Hiking and Backpacking

If you and your Malamute do not live in a winter climate, you can still enjoy the adventure of the outdoors together. Hiking is a great way to get your Malamute active and engaged. Backpacking with your Malamute involves your dog carrying a canine backpack while hiking through the woods.

Photo Courtesy of
Julie and Ric Edwards

Canine backpacking still requires training to get your dog accustomed to carrying the pack. Begin with getting an expert opinion on the type of pack your Malamute requires. Again, seek out local pack sellers or experienced backpackers. Once you have the proper pack, begin by putting it on your dog empty so he can get used to it. Once he adjusts, slowly begin adding weight, little by little, until he is eventually carrying the weight required for a hike. This training may take weeks to build up his endurance. Don't rush him or you may risk injury and further setbacks.

The Alaskan Malamute HELP League gives out Working Pack Dog (WPD) titles. If you are the competitive type, you may want to work toward earning this badge of honor.

WPD Requirements – According to the Alaskan Malamute HELP League at Malammuterescue.com

For a **Working Pack Dog title,** the packing requirements must be spread out over at least two trips, and must be on natural terrain, such as hiking trails or cross country. The dog must carry a weight equal to at least 30% of its own weight. You can choose between a total distance of 30 miles, including one overnight campout, or 40 miles, with each trip a minimum of 10 miles, as outlined below.

The dog must carry a **daily initial weight** equal to a minimum of 30% of its own weight. This weight shall not decrease except by normal consumption of items such as food or water.

Option 1: The dog must pack for a minimum of 30 miles. Each trip must be at least 10 miles per day or an overnight camp out with 5 miles in and 5 miles out. At least one trip must include an overnight camp out.

Option 2: The dog must pack for a minimum of 40 miles. Each trip must be at least 10 miles per day.

- Elevation gain may be substituted for mileage at the rate of 1,000 feet of elevation being equivalent to 1 mile of flat terrain. Elevation gain will be calculated as the difference between the highest and lowest points of the trip.

- Packing requirements shall be spread out over a minimum of 2 trips.

- An impartial witness must sign the form, verifying proof of distance and dog(s) competing.

Outdoor sport, no matter which you choose, is a great way to keep your Malamute occupied, engaged, and enjoying life. That is just the life an Alaskan Malamute would choose: one full of purpose, adventure, and plenty of human companionship and love.

CHAPTER 9
Training Your Alaskan Malamute

Consistency and Routine

"Frequency and consistency are the keys. If you tell a Malamute that you expect a certain response 10 times and they do it perfectly, and then on the 11th time if they do not respond correctly and you fail to correct them, then they feel that it's okay to not respond correctly. NEVER stop training."

Pat McGovern
ThunderKloud Alaskan Malamutes

Photo Courtesy of
Daniel and Karina Wheater

Consistency and routine are important in any dog's training, but even more so for an Alaskan Malamute. As previously discussed, Malamutes can make wonderful companions, but they are stubborn, independent and sometimes a little bit rebellious. These are not bad qualities that make your Malamute aggressive or defective; it's simply the way Alaskan Malamutes are hardwired.

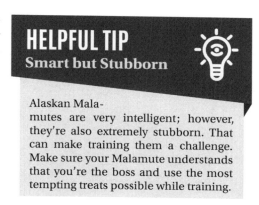

HELPFUL TIP
Smart but Stubborn

Alaskan Mala-mutes are very intelligent; however, they're also extremely stubborn. That can make training them a challenge. Make sure your Malamute understands that you're the boss and use the most tempting treats possible while training.

To successfully train a Malamute, you will need a firm hand, consistency and preferably lots of experience with the breed. If you give a Malamute an inch, he will try to take a mile. Enforcing the rules is critical! If you have never trained a Malamute and don't have the time or patience to tackle the job alone, consider hiring a professional. Not just any dog trainer will be a good fit for your Malamute, so be sure a person has breed specific experience before you hire them.

Benefits of Proper Training

Training your Malamute will be challenging and frustrating at times, but it will deepen the relationship between you and your dog. Training also serves an equally important purpose when it comes to safety. A properly trained Malamute will come when called and obey out of mutual trust and loyalty. This is particularly important in times of crisis or emergency. You should trust that your Malamute will understand and obey in stressful situations. That obedience may even save his life.

Alaskan Malamutes are a challenging breed, but it is possible to raise a well-mannered, obedient Malamute. Many owners successfully train their Malamutes to accompany them in public places like parks or outdoor restaurants with no problems at all. With some hard work and consistent training in the beginning, your Malamute can grow into the loyal, loving companion you have always wanted!

There are options when it comes to obedience training. You can search local advertisements and attend a group class, hire a personal trainer to come to your home, or train your dog yourself. No matter what you choose to do, be diligent and stick with the training schedule. The rewards of an obedient Malamute will pay off for years to come.

Training Methods

There are two main methods when it comes to training a dog: alpha dog training and positive reinforcement. Hotly debated among dog trainers, these two methods are vastly different. When choosing the method that is right for your dog, you must take some things into consideration and understand the details of each one.

Alpha Dog Training

Alpha training, popularized by television's dog trainer Cesar Millan, focuses on making yourself the alpha, or the leader of the pack. This training begins early by maintaining heavy control over your dog's actions. Users of this method are told to never allow a dog in bed, not to allow a dog to go through a doorway first, and never to get down at eye level with a dog. It's also advised that you touch your dog's food to place your scent on it before giving it to him and don't let him eat until you give the verbal okay.

Photo Courtesy of Rebeca Miranda

Proponents of this method claim that dogs are pack animals and need to have a sense of who is alpha in order to learn to submit. They claim that wolves assert their dominance over one another to keep each other in check. In reality, research has shown that wolves in the wild do not have such a rigid hierarchy. They live socially among each other much like humans do with their own families.

When it comes to obedience training, alpha training employs the use of restraints such as choke and shock collars and forceful body maneuvers. This method relies heavily on punishments and teaching your dog what he is doing wrong rather than teaching him how to do it right. While some trainers believe in the effectiveness of alpha training methods, others believe it is cruel and can actually undermine your relationship with your dog making it one based on fear and not trust.

Positive Reinforcement

The most recommended method of training today is positive reinforcement. The idea is that by reinforcing good behavior and obedience with desirable treats, your dog will both learn the commands and build trust with the trainer. It's still important to let your dog know that you are in control, but this is done through positive reinforcement rather than force. Bad behavior is not punished by harm or discomfort, rather it is ignored or redirected.

Dogs have been selectively bred over thousands of years to live alongside humans. Most dogs thrive on companionship and will do anything to please their people. Using positive reinforcement is a method of teaching them to understand what you want them to do and showing dogs that what makes you happy also makes them happy. This is the opposite of fear-based training and will build loyalty and trust naturally.

Which Method is Best for Your Malamute

It is important to understand that all breeds are different. While one breed may be naturally submissive and eager to please, another may be naturally dominant and bossy. When it comes to training your Malamute, there is a level of dominance that must be asserted over your dog. He will want to be the boss, it's just his nature! While you must never cause physical harm or discomfort to control your dog, a combination of Alpha training and positive reinforcement can be used to successfully train an Alaskan Malamute. Setting strict boundaries with your dog (such as not allowing him in your bed and putting your scent on his food before he eats) can help remind him that he is not your equal and may help lessen his natural desire to assert dominance. Remember, these dogs were bred to survive in the harsh wilderness and were allowed to keep many of their natural, wolf-like instincts.

Primary Reinforcement

Primary reinforcements are directly related to innate, basic needs. These can vary depending on breed and animal but always include things such as food and water. Training treats are a primary reinforcement successfully used in training.

Secondary Reinforcement

Secondary reinforcements are things not based on instinctual, basic need but rather are cultural constructs. This includes verbal praise, smiles, and pats. Your dog must learn to associate these actions positively by pairing them with primary reinforcements.

Another type of secondary reinforcement is conditioned reinforcement. This is when something neutral, such as a whistle or a clicker, is used in conjunction with a primary reinforcement to create a positive association. Conditioned reinforcements can be highly effective initially but can lose their effectiveness when the primary reinforcement is taken away for an extended period of time.

Dangers of Correcting Using Punishment

Photo Courtesy of Eryn Morgan

Correcting using punishment, such as with the use of shock collars and physical pain, has no scientific research backing it up as a legitimate training method. This type of forced control over a dog can lead to fear, anxiety, and can even put you or your family in danger. Using this method without an experienced professional's supervision can lead to a damaged relationship with your dog and a loss of trust.

Not only is this type of training risky, but it is also often ineffective. Instead of punishing your dog to stop him from doing what he isn't supposed to, show him what he is supposed to do and reward him for that. It may take a little bit longer to master, but your relationship will grow positively in the process. You can still successfully establish yourself as the dominant leader without asserting physical pain.

In the early stages of training, you may have to gently guide your Malamute into the desired behavior, and then give the treat. It is often said that a Malamute will love to please you – as long as it pleases him too! If you find that you're becoming frustrated and your Malamute is not cooperating, you may just need to take a step back and try again the next day.

Photo Courtesy of Jillian Taylor

Basic Commands

Obedience training is not just about learning to sit or shake. It's about building a mutual trust and respect between you and your Malamute and communicating your wishes in a way your dog can understand. In order to build this trust, though, you must begin by teaching your dog basic commands.

Photo Courtesy of Doris Thompson

Most obedience classes or personal trainers begin training by teaching a few easy, basic commands. These commands lay the foundation for more complicated tricks later. If you are choosing to train your dog yourself, follow the steps below to master these five basic commands.

Sit

The sit command is the easiest one to teach and can be learned in a short period of time. Take your dog to a calm area free of distractions like toys. Have a bag full of very small training treats ready. With your dog standing, facing you, hold a treat in front of his nose and slowly raise it up and over his head so he is guided to gradually sit down and look up. Give the verbal command "sit" as you do this. When he sits, reward him with a treat and a key phrase such as "yes" or "good." If you're training with a clicker, also give a click when he obeys the command.

Down

Once your dog has mastered the sit command, move on to the down command. Guide your dog into a seated position, facing you. Hold a treat in front of his nose, lower it to the floor, and give the verbal command "down." If your dog raises his backside to a standing position to retrieve the treat, take the treat away and say "no." Begin again from a seated position. When your dog successfully lies down to retrieve the treat, reward with a treat, a positive verbal cue such as "yes," and a click.

*Photo Courtesy of
Elizabeth Hendrix
Photo by Barbara O'Brien Photography*

Heel

Teaching your dog to heel requires him to walk on your left side at your pace whenever you're out and about. The heel command is a bit challenging and requires significant focus from your dog. He must stop when you stop and walk when you walk, never stepping in front of your left heel. This command is great for preventing leash tugging.

Begin by having your dog sit in front, facing you. Using your left hand, let your dog smell the treat and then swing your arm around to the left, luring your dog to turn around and stop in a position next to you but slightly behind, facing the same direction you are. Reward your dog immediately when he arrives in the correct position. Use the command "heel." Repeat this command many times, always having your dog come to the heel position before rewarding him.

After your dog has mastered the heel position, progress by taking a few steps using the same verbal "heel" command. Reward your dog for walking with you in the correct position. If your dog leaves the correct heel position, guide him back to where he is supposed to be before continuing.

Stay

To teach your dog to stay, command him to sit, facing you. With a visible treat in hand, hold up your palm to your dog and say "stay." Take one step backward. If your dog doesn't move, quickly return and reward him. You don't want your dog leaving the stay position to retrieve the treat. If your dog moves, say "no" and return him to a sitting position. As your dog gets the hang of "stay," increase the number of steps.

Leave It

This command is valuable and can help keep your dog safe if he gets into something potentially dangerous. Begin with two treats, one in each hand. Keep one hand in a fist but allow your dog to sniff the treat. As your dog tries to get into your hand to get the treat, verbally command him to "leave it." Repeat this command until your dog backs off and then reward with the treat from the other hand. As your dog progresses, make the treat more accessible and challenge your pup to leave it in exchange for another treat.

Once you and your Malamute have successfully mastered these basic commands, you will be well on your way to owning a well-mannered dog. Just remember, Malamutes have a mind of their own, so don't get too frustrated when you want him to show off all his new tricks and he suddenly acts as if he's never heard a single one. That is the wonderful, hilarious, and sometimes challenging life of a Malamute owner!

When and How to Hire a Trainer

If you are training at home but are having trouble making progress, it may be time to hire a professional trainer. Training a Malamute takes a lot of time and consistency and it is easy to get frustrated, sending your dog mixed messages while training. If the mixed signals go on for too long, it can cause major setbacks in your dog's progress. The quicker you can address the issue of a rebellious Malamute, the easier it will be to correct the behavior.

If you are dealing with any kind of aggression or poor social behaviors that do not seem to be improving, hire a trainer specialized in that area to help you get through to your dog. If you think you need help from a professional trainer, don't put it off. The sooner your dog is properly trained the sooner you can live together in peaceful companionship.

Owner Expectations

"Don't listen when people say Malamutes are stubborn and hard to teach. Malamutes are smart; just make the training interesting by playing with them and training at intervals."

Randy Checketts
Chex Alaskan Malamutes

No matter where you choose to begin obedience training, you should have clear expectations so you can be prepared for the amount of work it will take to successfully train your dog. You play as big a role in obedience training as your dog does, even if you don't choose to do the training yourself.

Obedience Classes

Obedience classes, either private or group, are usually held about once or twice a week. Most facilities require you to provide vaccination records before a dog will be allowed to start training. Obedience training typically begins at about six months of age but dog ages in a class can vary widely. It is never too late to begin obedience training, so even if you have adopted a senior Malamute, he's not too old to learn!

Before your first training session, ask for a list of materials you will need to bring. The facility will likely require your dog to have a leash and may ask you to provide your own training treats. Most obedience classes require a name tag with identification, and some require a clicker. By purchasing all necessary supplies before class day, you can ensure that all your time is spent learning from the trainer and not scrambling to get what you need.

Even if classes are only held twice a week, be prepared to spend at least 15-20 minutes daily working on what your dog has learned. Just as with any skill, obedience training takes practice and repetition. It may not be easy, but this training will reinforce to your dog the idea that you are his pack leader.

CHAPTER 10
Dealing with Unwanted Behaviors

Malamute owners know that dealing with unwanted behavior just comes with the territory. It's a sacrifice they are willing to make in order to own and love a breed as special as the Alaskan Malamute.

What Is Considered Bad Behavior in Dogs?

We all want a well-trained, obedient dog, but even successful training won't keep a spunky dog from being spunky. Just like humans, dogs can exhibit behaviors that are annoying at times but that doesn't necessarily mean they are bad. So, when it comes to bad habits and behaviors, what is actually considered "bad"?

Howling or Barking: Malamutes are a relatively quiet breed in general and they don't often bark. They do, however, "talk" and howl. Howling is as natural for your dog as speaking is to you and should never be considered bad behavior. In fact, many Malamute owners find this "woo woo" to be an endearing trait; one that some have even made viral on the internet!

Photo Courtesy of Irene Russell

*Photo Courtesy of
Brooke Hanley*

If your dog is particularly chatty and "talks" or howls a bit too frequently, there are measures you can take to correct the annoyance. First, try to find the root cause of the vocalization. Is there a direct, consistent trigger such as seeing other people or dogs? If this is the case, socialization may be in order to give your dog a chance to engage with other pups in an appropriate setting. If the problem is more sporadic and inconsistent, consider whether your Malamute may simply be trying to get your attention. Are you spending enough one on one time with your dog? These dogs have extremely high energy needs, mentally and physically, and the noise issue may be a result of those needs not being met.

If your Malamute still howls at inappropriate times, you might try a simple preventative measure. Take an empty aluminum beverage can, fill it with coins or nuts and bolts, and seal the top with tape. If the dog howls inappropriately (without a normal trigger), rattle the can and use a verbal prompt like "Quiet!" The noise made by the can will startle the dog, and he will come to associate the prompt word with the noise. Be sure to praise and comfort your Malamute when he stops howling. This is a variation of negative reinforcement that does not involve any physical discomfort or pain.

Photo Courtesy of
Betty Ladd

Chasing – Cats, bunnies, and other animals beware! Malamutes are born chasers. A natural prey drive exists more strongly in Alaskan Malamutes than in other breeds. While this behavior can become an issue, it should never be treated as "bad." Your Malamute is only doing what comes naturally to him. Obedience training can help this issue but may not eliminate it completely.

Digging – As discussed in a previous chapter, Malamutes are also born diggers. They just can't seem to help themselves! Much like chasing, digging is a natural behavior and may involve rolling around the freshly disturbed dirt. This is not bad behavior but can become annoying and may be curbed with stricter supervision and obedience training.

Leash Pulling – This is a direct result of improper or inadequate training and is not bad behavior. Teach your dog the proper way to walk on a leash with the help of a trainer and this annoyance can be eliminated altogether.

Other unwanted behaviors that are not "bad" include chewing up toys or shoes that were left out, begging for or stealing food, jumping on people, getting on furniture, and eating poop. All of these behaviors can be a nuisance but are typically not evidence of a poorly behaved dog.

Aggression – Behavior that should always be considered "bad" is any form of unprovoked aggression. This could be vicious growling, biting, lunging, or snarling. These behaviors are unacceptable and if not dealt with immediately, can result in serious injury or death for your dog or the object of his aggression. This includes food or possession aggression. Aggression can be common among Malamutes so seek professional help quickly if the behavior arises.

Finding the Root of the Problem

When dealing with any unwanted behavior, the first step to eliminating the issue is finding the root cause. Learning the why will make correcting the problem so much easier for both you and your dog. Unfortunately, for a Malamute, there may not be a specific trigger. Some of these instincts still exist naturally in the Alaskan Malamute. This does not make your dog "bad," but it will make him more challenging to control.

Instinctual – If the unwanted behavior you are dealing with is something instinctually bred into your dog, it will probably be more difficult to correct. Try training with a professional, but if that doesn't work you may have to redirect the unwanted behavior into an appropriate outlet. For example, if your dog loves to chase, find a way for him to chase safely in a controlled environment, such as using a flirt pole. This type of approach applies to all instinctual issues including chewing and digging. Allow your dog to do these natural things in a way that prevents him from do-

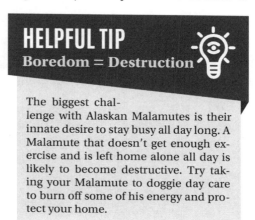

HELPFUL TIP
Boredom = Destruction

The biggest challenge with Alaskan Malamutes is their innate desire to stay busy all day long. A Malamute that doesn't get enough exercise and is left home alone all day is likely to become destructive. Try taking your Malamute to doggie day care to burn off some of his energy and protect your home.

Photo Courtesy of
Lucy Bottcher

ing them in an inappropriate manner that may result in damaged or destroyed property.

Lack of Training – The majority of a dog's unwanted behaviors stem from a simple lack of training. Leash tugging, jumping, stealing food, and jumping on furniture are all a direct result of inconsistent boundaries set by the owner. Training your dog consistently and purposefully is the best way to correct these unwanted behaviors.

If you are dealing with a true aggression issue with your dog, determine what the root cause might be. Could he be suffering from a health issue? Is there a traumatic event in your dog's past? A longstanding lack of socialization? If so, there may be a long road of recovery ahead for your Malamute and you will more than likely require the assistance of a highly qualified trainer and possibly a dog psychologist. These behavioral issues can be a matter of life or death for a dog, especially one as large and powerful as a Malamute, so approach them with intention.

How to Properly Correct Your Dog

When it comes to correcting a Malamute, one thing is clear: you must be firm and consistent. Unless your Malamute has a deep-seated issue involving a traumatic past or mental condition, he will not wish to cause you any harm. Correct him by showing him what you want him to do instead of the unwanted behavior.

If it's an issue that does not concern safety, do your best to meet your dog in the middle with a solution that will make you both happy. If he loves to chew, keep a steady supply of interesting chew toys at his disposal so that he can still chew but you don't have to worry about your belongings. Even when meeting your dog in the middle with a solution, you must remain established as pack leader. You make the rules, he follows.

When to Call a Professional

Sometimes, even seemingly harmless unwanted behaviors can become a dangerous issue for your dog. Digging can be harmless if it only leads to holes in the backyard, but if it evolves into digging under the fence, it can become a serious problem quickly, exposing your dog to the many dangers that lie outside the fence, and exposing other animals to the dangers of your dog. Likewise, losing a few pairs of shoes to a chewer can be frustrating but not dangerous to your dog. However, if that chewer decides to eat a loose electrical cord or a toy with small batteries, it could end in an emergency trip to the animal hospital.

If your attempts to redirect your dog's behavior have been futile and you cannot get your Malamute under control, contact your local dog training facility and ask for help. They will undoubtedly have seen these issues before and will have the resources and tools to help you find a solution. It's important to seek help at the first sign of a problem and not let unwanted habits form. If you wait and habits do form, it will be much more challenging to correct the behavior down the road.

CHAPTER 11
Traveling with Your Alaskan Malamute

Deciding whether or not to travel with your Malamute can be a tough decision. We all want to take our fluffy companions with us wherever we go, but traveling can put unneeded stress on a dog. This chapter will explain all the ins and outs of traveling with your Malamute to help you make the best decision for you and your dog.

Flying with Your Malamute

Flying with your Malamute will take a lot of planning beforehand. There are only so many pets allowed on each airplane (this varies by airline and size of the plane) so you need to book your flight as early as possible to obtain a spot. In the past, airlines treated cargo animals just like any other lug-

Photo Courtesy of Joseph Bernard

Photo Courtesy of Hannah Smith

gage. Dogs were often left traumatized and sometimes even died because of temperature, lack of water, etc. Luckily, today, airlines have begun enforcing regulations to keep animals housed in the cargo area as safe and happy as possible.

Due to the size of an Alaskan Malamute, your dog will most likely not be allowed to fly in the passenger area, but instead will have to be checked in a crate into the cargo area. Most airlines charge a fee for transporting animals. It is usually somewhere between $75-$200 each way. If at all possible, you will want to get a direct flight for you and your Malamute. No matter how much airlines have worked to improve the process for animals, it will still be traumatizing for your dog and does carry a bit of risk.

Not all airlines follow the same guidelines for flying animals. Some require a certificate of veterinary inspection (CVI) before flying. Make sure you do thorough research on each airline before deciding on the best for you and your Malamute. Federal regulations prohibit any pets under eight weeks old from flying.

When it comes to airline approved kennels, technology and regulations are constantly changing. Check your local airline for their current recommendations on preferred kennels and read consumer reviews. Choosing a safe and sturdy kennel for your Malamute is one of the most important decisions you will make when deciding to fly with your dog.

Hotel Stays with Your Malamute

If you plan to stay in a hotel with your dog, there are a few things you need to look for before choosing. Not all hotels are pet friendly and some have size and breed restrictions. Before booking, check their website to be sure that large dogs are allowed. Checking online for the highest rated pet-friendly hotels is a great place to start.

When deciding on a hotel, make sure it has adequate outdoor space for your Malamute. Not all hotels allow pets and even then, sometimes a hotel may consider itself "pet friendly" but may not have much to offer in the way of pet amenities. Look for a hotel with a fenced dog run with adequate space for your Malamute to let off a bit of energy.

Photo Courtesy of
Jillian Taylor

You may also want to request a room on the ground floor. This will make it easier for you to access the bathroom area designated for your dog. Some hotels are known for designating the older, outdated or smoking rooms as pet rooms. Before booking, call and ask if the pet rooms are any different than other rooms.

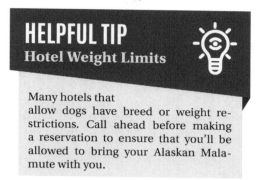

HELPFUL TIP
Hotel Weight Limits

Many hotels that allow dogs have breed or weight restrictions. Call ahead before making a reservation to ensure that you'll be allowed to bring your Alaskan Malamute with you.

Bring a kennel when staying in a hotel just in case you have to leave your Malamute unattended for any period of time. Some hotels don't allow pets to be alone, so make sure you check beforehand. Even if you don't plan on using the kennel, you never know when something might come up and you don't want your Malamute to cause any damage in the room alone.

Kenneling vs. Dog Sitters

If you are choosing to travel without your dog, you will need to decide what to do with him while you are away. There are two basic choices for care while you are gone. You can put your dog at a boarding kennel until you return, or you can hire a dog-sitter. Depending on your needs and the personality of your dog, either of these can be a great option!

If you won't be gone for an extended period of time, you may find hiring a dog sitter a more affordable option. This is typically when you hire someone to come and take your dog out 2-3 times a day and make sure he has food and water. This may be a professional dog sitter or a trusted friend or family member. Because Malamutes require so much exercise, this is only a good option for a day or two. After this, your Malamute may begin to feel cooped up and anxious, possibly becoming destructive.

For most Malamutes that get along well with other dogs, finding a good boarding kennel will be the best option. Most of these places allow your dog to play with other dogs in a safe environment for most of the day. This can be like a vacation for your dog!

Choosing the Right Boarding Facility

All boarding facilities are different and come with their own rules and benefits. They can range from basic, small, cage-like kennels to full sized dog rooms with elevated beds and doggy doors to an outside patio. Nice boarding facilities will have a common area inside and out where the dogs can play together. Price can vary drastically depending on location but can range between $20-$60 a night.

Never take your dog to a boarder that does not require the Bordetella vaccine. These places can be a breeding ground for kennel cough, so make sure you plan for your dog to get the vaccine at least two weeks before his visit.

Check out local boarding facilities online before choosing and check consumer reviews. Ask your local pet store or vet and see which they do and don't recommend. Most facilities charge a price per night and will often have different levels of service. Often times these places will allow you to choose between a private or shared room and some even have televisions with DogTV. You may even be able to watch a live stream of your Malamute while he is playing with his new buddies.

Whichever route you choose, make sure you trust your choice and that your dog is well taken care of while you are away. The last thing you want to do is worry about your dog while you are away.

Photo Courtesy of Michelle Irwin

Photo Courtesy of
Kelsey Holowati

Special Tips and Tricks for Traveling

"As long as they are crate trained and can ride in a crate, they are great travel companions. Most Malamutes do not get car sick and they love to meet new people and explore new places."

Pat McGovern
ThunderKloud Alaskan Malamute

Traveling with your Malamute can be fun and exciting, but it can also be stressful! Follow these tips to help any trip with your loyal companion a stress free one!

- Don't feed your Malamute within 4 hours of any trip. This includes car rides, plane rides, and any other method of transportation. This may help prevent you having to clean up vomit.

- Exercise your Malamute vigorously the day before and the day of your trip. Let him get as much energy out as he possibly can before being put into his crate.

127

Photo Courtesy of Kaitlyn Sutton

- Don't sedate your dog! This once common practice is no longer recommended by veterinarians. Sedating a dog can inhibit his ability to react in an emergency and is simply not good for his health.

- Check in as late as possible at the airport so your Malamute doesn't have to spend the extra time waiting.

- If you are flying, make sure that your rental car or car service allows for dogs to ride.

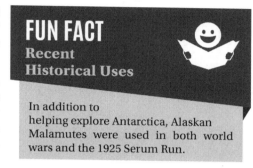

FUN FACT

Recent Historical Uses

In addition to helping explore Antarctica, Alaskan Malamutes were used in both world wars and the 1925 Serum Run.

- Always have a bowl, leash, water, and plastic waste bags with you. No matter how you are traveling, these basic items will be daily necessities. If you're driving, stop often to let your dog potty and keep him hydrated.

- Always have the number to a local an emergency vet on hand. Emergencies can happen anywhere, so look up local animal hospitals before you travel just in case!

CHAPTER 12
Nutrition

Importance of Good Diet

"Malamutes can have sensitive stomachs. Drinking too much water or over eating (they like to eat) can cause upset stomach and lead to diarrhea or vomiting."

Gail Partain
Windwalker Malamutes

When it comes to feeding ourselves, we know that there are some foods that are better for us than others. For the sake of our health, we do our best to eat a balanced diet and avoid processed foods with harmful additives. These same rules apply when it comes to feeding our Malamutes. Just like humans, dogs need a certain balance of protein, fats, carbohydrates, vitamins, and minerals to keep their bodies going.

All commercial dog foods have been tested rigorously and are required to meet minimum nutritional requirements. Although this is true, minimum requirements are not what is best for your dog's health long term. Feeding your dog low-quality dog food is the equivalent of feeding him processed junk food. Choosing a dog food that is made with the best ingredients and does not include preservatives and additives will help your dog function at his optimal level, including his immune system, potentially protecting against disease.

According to Dr. Hugh Stevenson, a veterinarian in Ontario, Canada, for over twenty years, poor nutrition can be noted by a dull, thin coat, poor quality foot pads (which can crack or bleed), weight problems, excess stool and gas, and passing undigested grain particles in feces. Quality dog nutrition leads to a lustrous coat, healthy skin and weight, and less stool due to more of the food being digested. When it comes to your Malamute companion, a quality food will give him the best possible start from puppyhood on.

The Pros and Cons of Commercial Dog Food

There are many dog foods that claim to be the best, healthiest, and most complete. It can be both overwhelming and confusing. Should you buy dry kibble? Canned wet food? Each contains a different list of ingredients and promises on the label, so how do you really know what you're getting?

The first choice you will have to make is whether to feed your Malamute dry kibble or wet food. Each choice comes with its own set of positives and negatives.

Wet Dog Food: Wet dog food has a very strong smell. This may be a positive for a dog who is particularly picky or doesn't have much interest in eating as the strong scent may entice him to eat. It could also be a negative if you don't want to smell the food in your home every time you feed your Malamute. Wet food also helps with hydration if you have a dog that doesn't drink as much as he should, but it spoils quickly after opening. If your dog doesn't finish his food promptly, you'll need to store the rest in the refrigerator. Canned food can also be a bit messier to eat, depending on your dog. Feeding a dog the size of an Alaskan Malamute wet food is also an expensive choice. Wet dog food costs, on average, eighty-five cents more per pound than dry.

Dry Dog Food: Dry dog food is easier to store once opened because it doesn't spoil when left out. This is beneficial for a dog who may like to come

back to his food throughout the day. Dry dog food also doesn't have much of a smell so it can sit out in your home without anyone noticing. Some dry kibble has been formulated to help clean your dog's teeth while he chews although some experts say the added grains in certain dry foods contribute to tooth decay. If you choose dry food, make doubly sure your Malamute has ready access to water throughout the day, since kibble does not provide any hydration.

Whichever type of food you choose for your dog, it's important to remember that both canned food and kibble exists in low quality forms. Low quality brands include cheap fillers, artificial colors, flavors, and preservatives and should be avoided.

Ingredients to Avoid

It can be confusing reading the ingredient list on a dog food label. Companies that produce low quality dog food use vague terms and scientific words to try and make you think a product contains quality, wholesome ingredients when it may not. Below is a list of key ingredients to avoid when searching for the best commercial dog food for your Malamute.

BHA/ BHT

Studies are not conclusive, but these chemical preservatives have been linked to hyperactivity and cancer. Used to preserve fats in human food and pet food, BHA and BHT have been banned in some countries but are still allowed in the United States, Canada, and Europe. Until conclusive evidence proves these preservatives are safe, it's best to avoid them altogether.

Meat, Meat Meal, or Rendered Fat

Any time you see a vague, non-specific term such as "meat" or "meat meal," you can bet these are the lowest quality ingredients allowed. These ingredients are leftovers from slaughterhouses; the parts humans won't eat. It can also include leftover, expired meats from the grocery store, and diseased and dying livestock. Instead, look for specific meat terms you recognize such as turkey, beef, salmon, lamb, or chicken.

If your dog food contains salmon or salmon meal, make sure it's labeled "wild caught." Farm raised salmon is less nutrient dense than its wild counterpart because of the unnatural diet the fish are fed and has been found to potentially contain more contaminants.

Photo Courtesy of
Debra Gallagher

Nitrites and Nitrates

Chemical additives used to preserve freshness and extend the shelf life of meat products, nitrates and nitrites are found in human and dog food. Sodium nitrite can be toxic to your dog in high doses and has been linked to cancer.

Soy

Soy is cheap and readily available. Dog food manufacturers may use it as an inexpensive way to boost the protein percentage of a food, but it can be difficult to digest for your dog and can cause gastrointestinal upset.

Other ingredients to avoid include meat by-products, sodium hexametaphosphate, food dyes, carrageenan, taurine, cellulose, artificial flavors, and corn syrup. Dog food manufacturers dedicated to producing a quality, superior dog food will not contain these red flag ingredients. Though they can be a bit more expensive, the cost will be well worth it and may even save you money in vet bills in the long term by nourishing your Malamute properly.

There has been a recent trend toward grain-free dog food. Some claim that because wolves in the wild don't consume more than a trace amount of grains, domesticated dogs shouldn't either. The truth is, dogs are not genetically identical to wolves and they have adapted to effectively utilize grains.

In fact, grain-free dog food often contains other plants instead of grains. These are usually peas, lentils, potatoes, and legumes. These plant sources provide the starch to make the kibble as well as an added protein boost, allowing the manufacturer to cut back on the more expensive animal proteins. This can lead to a depletion of the amino acid taurine. Taurine is found in animal proteins, but not in plant proteins and the FDA has linked this to a rise of cardiomyopathy in dogs that have been fed a grain-free diet. While the verdict is still out on grain-free dog food, it is best to discuss with your vet what food is best for your Malamute before jumping on the grain-free trend.

Homemade Dog Food

Some owners choose to skip commercial dog food altogether and make their dog's meals themselves instead. This is the only real way to know exactly what your Malamute is eating. If you have the time and resources, homemade dog food can provide your Malamute with a wonderful source of balanced nutrition including real, whole foods and none of the preservatives found in commercial foods. In addition, food prepared at home contains more nutrients than processed food. This is because the high temperature used during processing causes significant loss of nutrients.

Photo Courtesy of Nathan Martin

Many homemade dog food recipes can be found online, but it's very important that you discuss specific recipes with your vet to be sure they provide your dog with all of the nutrients he needs. Individual breeds and even dogs of the same breed can have different nutritional needs. When making your dog's food yourself, it's important to get a professional opinion regarding ingredients and serving size.

Many owners are also opting to feed their dogs a raw diet. While controversial, proponents tout various health benefits. Discuss this option with your vet before making the switch. Just as with any other homemade dog food, making sure you include everything your dog needs is the most important thing.

Giving Your Dog Human Food

When it comes to feeding your dog human food, the key to safety is knowing what is beneficial and what is not. In Chapter 3 we already discussed a list of foods to never feed your Malamute, so you may want to return there and refresh your memory before continuing on to this list of foods that are okay to share with your pup. Remember, feeding your dog directly from the table can quickly form bad habits, such as begging. This may be cute the first time but may get old fast when you want to enjoy a meal in peace.

There are a number of things you can safely share with your dog from your kitchen as a special treat or snack, but remember that these should be given in moderation so they don't upset the balance of your dog's nutrition. None of these items should be heavily seasoned as this may cause an upset stomach.

- White and brown rice
- Cooked eggs
- Oatmeal
- Carrots
- Cheese
- Peanut butter (without xylitol)
- Berries
- Green beans
- Seedless watermelon
- Bananas
- Peas
- Pineapple
- Apples
- Broccoli
- Potatoes

This is not a comprehensive list and food sensitivities can differ from dog to dog so consult your veterinarian if you think your dog may have a food allergy or sensitivity.

Photo Courtesy of Magdalena Lewandowska

Weight Management

There are two easy tests you can do to determine if your Malamute is overweight:

1. Run your hand gently along your dog's side. You should be able to feel the rib cage under a light layer of fat.

2. While your dog is standing, look at him from above. You should see a narrowing at the waist, just behind the rib cage.

If your Malamute is overweight, you should deal with the problem immediately. Begin by implementing a more active routine. Malamutes require a lot of physical activity and without it can quickly become overweight. Consult Chapter 8 for ideas to make exercise fun for you and your Malamute.

Also consider where your dog is getting his nutrition. Is he eating a quality commercial food? Low quality foods contain filler ingredients that will fill your dog up temporarily but don't provide adequate nutrients. Your dog may end up eating more of these foods to make up for the lack of nutrition, causing weight issues. If you prepare homemade dog food for your pup, you may need to go back to the vet or nutritionist to reevaluate ingredients and portion sizes.

What is your dog eating when it isn't mealtime? Are you sharing too many snacks from the kitchen with your Malamute? Moderation is the key to sharing special treats and too many can be detrimental to your dog's health if it leads to obesity and disease. If weight is an issue for your Malamute, cut out the snacks all together and feed him only at designated mealtimes.

If you can't get your dog's weight under control by limiting snacks and providing a quality commercial food, dis-

HELPFUL TIP
Weight Matters

Between their stocky shape and thick fur, it can be difficult to tell if Malamutes are overweight. More than half of all pet dogs are overweight, and obesity causes many of the same health problems in dogs as it does in people. How can you tell if your Malamute is overweight? You should be able to feel his ribs without too much trouble. If you can't feel your dog's ribs, talk to your vet about how to get your dog to a healthy weight.

cuss options with your vet. He or she may suggest a weight management food. These foods feature higher than average protein, lower than average fat, and fewer calories. These foods are formulated for adult dogs only and should never be given to a puppy. Remember to read food labels and choose a food made with high-quality ingredients.

CHAPTER 13
Basic Healthcare and Grooming

Visiting the Vet

Aside from the first vet visit, discussed in Chapter 4, your Alaskan Malamute should see the vet routinely for check-ups and vaccinations. At these regular visits your vet will examine your Malamute from tip to tail. This should include listening to the heart and lungs and examining the ears, eyes, nose, and mouth. It should also involve an abdominal examination for any abnormalities. The vet may also draw blood to check for heartworms and take a stool sample to check for other parasites. Sometimes the vet will examine your dog's gait and coat condition. Be ready to answer any questions about diet or your dog's daily routine. Malamutes are susceptible to many genetic conditions so it is important to keep up with annual wellness checks with your vet so you can catch anything early before it becomes a bigger issue.

Photo Courtesy of
Brent Rudmann

Vaccinations

Vaccinations prevent diseases by injecting the body with antigens to elicit an immune response producing antibodies for those diseases. The vaccinations cause no symptoms of disease but do give the body time to recognize and build up an immunity so that if the dog comes into contact with a virus, his immune system will respond swiftly. Vaccinations are an important part in keeping your dog safe from potentially life-threatening illnesses.

A puppy will receive antibodies from its mother's milk for at least the first 6 weeks of its life and should be protected from many illnesses that way. Distemper, Adenovirus, Hepatitis, Parvovirus, and Parainfluenza are considered the core vaccinations that ev-

Photo Courtesy of Jesse Ortega

ery puppy should receive at 6 weeks of age. These shots are usually given in 4 rounds: once at 6 weeks, 10 weeks, 14 weeks, and 18 weeks. Most vets administer these core shots in a combination vaccine called a 5-Way. Depending on your area, some vets will recommend additional vaccinations. These may include Bordetella, Leptospirosis, and Coronavirus.

The rabies vaccine is always administered separately and is recommended no earlier than 12 weeks. While some veterinarians may want to give the vaccine in addition to other combo vaccinations at your Malamute's second-round appointment, some breeders strongly suggest no more than one vaccine be given in a single visit. Depending on where you live, legally your dog will be required to receive a rabies vaccine every 1 to 3 years.

Reactions to these vaccines are rare but possible. Sometimes vaccinations can trigger an allergic reaction causing swelling, hives, vomiting, and fever. If your dog does have a reaction, notify your vet immediately. Even if the reaction is mild, make sure the vet is aware before your dog is given more vaccinations. The benefits of vaccinations far outweigh the risks. These vaccinations are one of the best ways to help set your dog up for a long, healthy life.

Fleas and Ticks

Photo Courtesy of Karen Aldridge

Fleas are the most common external parasite to afflict dogs and they are a problem almost everywhere. They reproduce quickly and a single female flea can lay 20-40 eggs a day. If your Malamute picks up a flea or two from the park and he has not been protected from fleas, you could be dealing with an infestation in your home before you know it.

Ticks can go largely unnoticed by their host, but they can cause a much bigger health problem than fleas. Ticks are notorious for transmitting dangerous diseases to dogs, humans, and other animals. While most ticks prefer your furry Malamute as a host, they won't hesitate to also latch on to you if they get the opportunity.

Flea and tick prevention is important for your dog's health and for your own. There are many options when it comes to prevention and it is important you understand the benefits and the disadvantages of each one before you choose which is best for your dog.

One common flea and tick preventative is administered topically. Typically, this medication comes in a small tube that the owner squeezes onto the dog's back between the shoulder blades. This topical medication usually takes about 12 hours to take effect and will last about 30 days before it needs to be reapplied. This works because the solution is absorbed into the skin and circulates through the dog's blood stream, treating fleas and ticks over the entire body, not just the area it was directly applied. One disadvantage of this application is it usually leaves a greasy spot on your dog's back for a few days. Considering this is a medication, it is probably not something you want to touch yourself or allow children to come in contact with.

It is important to note that topical treatments should never be used on a young puppy. In order to prevent adverse reactions, make sure to read the minimum age recommendations on the label, and consult with your vet before applying these.

Another method of administration is oral medication. There are numerous tablets on the market that prevent fleas and tick for 30 days. Some of these prevent heartworms and internal parasites as well. Depending on how your dog does with medication, this could be an easier way to prevent the parasites without the mess of topical application. As with any medications, side effects do exist. While they are generally mild, some dogs can react with skin irritations, vomiting, or diarrhea.

You can also buy a special flea collar for your dog. These are collars worn in addition to your dog's identification collar. They are covered topical flea medications, usually Permethrin. This provides long lasting protection for your dog, up to 8 months, but can cause skin irritation for your dog. While these collars have been deemed safe for dogs, permethrin can cause toxicity in cats and is believed to be a carcinogen in humans. Just like with the topical medication, children and adults should avoid contact with the active ingredients on flea collars. Flea collars should never be used on a young puppy.

Even if your Malamute lives primarily inside, he should be on a flea and tick preventative. It only takes one exposure to these parasites to spell bad news for you and your dog. It is much better to take preventative measures than to have to deal with the fleas or ticks after they have hitched a ride into your home.

If your Malamute scratches excessively and you suspect that he might have fleas, you can purchase a flea comb at any pet store. Flea combs have very fine and closely spaced teeth that fleas cannot pass between. Run the flea comb over your dog's body at a 45-degree angle, focusing on the areas where fleas are common (head, neck, hind quarters). If you see a flea caught in the comb, cover it quickly with your finger and trap it in a wet paper towel. This will restrain, but not kill, the flea, so the paper towel will have to be disposed of outside the house.

You may also give your dog a flea bath. Vacuum your entire house from the floor to the curtains. Anything upholstered is potentially a place where a flea

has laid eggs. If you notice fleas in your home, continue the vacuuming regimen twice a day for two weeks in order to get rid of all the fleas as they hatch.

If you find a tick on your dog, remove it immediately. Always wear gloves when removing a tick. Ticks carry serious diseases and you don't want to come into contact with their saliva or risk being bitten yourself. Once you have your gloves on, use a clean pair of tweezers and grab the tick firmly as close to the skin as possible. Pull firmly, straight up. You don't want to leave any of the mouth parts behind or this could lead to infection. Once you have removed the tick, place it in a jar of alcohol or soapy water. Keep the tick for identification by the vet in case your dog shows any symptoms of illness. Symptoms can take two weeks to surface so keep an eye out. Clean the bite thoroughly with antiseptic and watch the area for signs of irritation.

Coat Basics

The Alaskan Malamute has a thick double coat to keep him warm in those frigid Alaskan winters. Shedding is a year round issue for Malamutes, but they will also "blow" their coat twice a year. When this happens, your Malamute will lose mountains of fur in a short period of time so make sure to have the vacuum handy!

Bathing and Brushing

"You will need a rake brush that will get down in their coats to keep them from getting matted. Brush them as often as you can and feel their coat all over to make sure there are no matts forming. Never shave them thinking it will make them cooler in the summer time .That will only make them hotter."

Loretta Roach
Mountain Ridge Malamutes

Alaskan Malamutes need regular brushing to keep their thick coats clean and free from mats. Invest in a good quality slicker brush or bristle brush and use it daily. To keep your Malamute's coat in tip-top shape, you will want to bathe him every 1-6 weeks.

Improper coat care can lead to cobweb matting close to the skin which can cause serious skin conditions. Because of Malamutes' heavy double coats, proper washing and drying techniques are important to keep the coat shiny and soft.

Before bathing your Malamute, use a blow dryer to blow any excess dirt or hair off his coat. Keep the dryer far enough off the coat to avoid causing tangles. Once this is done, proceed with shampooing your dog's coat.

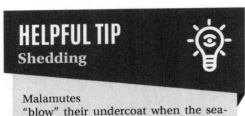

HELPFUL TIP
Shedding

Malamutes "blow" their undercoat when the seasons change, about two to four times per year. During these times, they will shed a lot and require extra brushing. When the undercoat starts coming out in clumps, a professional groomer can help remove most of that fur all at once so it doesn't end up all over your home. Never shave a Malamute—it can destroy their coat, and their fur keeps them cool better than the sun beating down directly on their skin.

When shampooing your Malamute, you will want to use a quality dog shampoo. Ask around local vets and groomers to see what they recommend. Never use human shampoo or conditioner on your Malamute. It is best to do this with a hand sprayer, but a large rinsing cup will do if that is all you have.

Make sure you clean the coat all the way down to the skin. Rinse with cool water and then use a towel to blot dry. Don't use the town to rub him dry because this will only cause tangles and mats to form in his coat.

Finish drying with a hair dryer and use the bristle brush to remove any tangles. Once finished, check the consistency of the coat with your hands. If one area feels more dense, go back over that area with the brush to remove any mats.

Due to the high maintenance nature of the Malamute's coat, you may consider taking him for a monthly trip to the groomers. Never, ever let them

cut your Malamutes beautiful coat, instead get him a professional wash, brush, and dry. Make sure you choose a groomer who has experience with the breed so you can be sure your dog's coat is handled properly.

Dental Care

Dental health is often overlooked when it comes to dogs, but proper oral care is important! Dogs can suffer from the same oral diseases and pains that humans do. Your dog should be taken to the vet every year or two for a professional dental cleaning. Talk to your vet about how often he or she recommends.

At home, brush your dog's teeth with a dog-specific toothpaste often to prevent any oral issues down the road. Never use human toothpaste, which is full of additives that are meant to be spit out (something your dog can't do). Brush gently and take it slow until your dog is accustomed to the toothbrush. If your dog is skeptical, start with toothpaste on your finger and gently touch his teeth. It is a good idea to do this once a week at the same time you brush his coat to create a routine.

Bushing is not the only way to help your Malamute keep his teeth in good shape. Chewing has been shown to naturally reduce plaque and tartar build-up. When using dental chews, it is advisable to always supervise your dog and remove the chew if it becomes a choking hazard.

Nail Trimming

"Keep the bottom of the feet trimmed of hair so they don't slip on flooring and keep the nails trimmed short. Long nails that drag on the floor weaken the pasterns."

Pat McGovern
ThunderKloud Alaskan Malamutes

Some people opt to have a groomer or a veterinarian trim their dog's nails but you can easily do this at home. You will need to invest in a quality nail trimmer. There are several types to choose from, including grinders, but they will all get the job done so choose based on your preference and what is easiest for you to maneuver. You should also purchase some styptic powder. This will stop any bleeding if you accidentally cut a nail too short.

Most clippers will come with instructions on how to clip the nails and it is important to follow them carefully to avoid injury to your dog.

Introduce the nail clippers to your Malamute early and often. Let your dog explore and sniff the clippers so he can get familiar with them. Hold them down to his feet and show him that they are not a threat. Reward him with treats to create a positive association. Do this often, even when your Malamute doesn't need a nail trim. This will help him to stay relaxed when it is time for an actual nail trimming session.

A dog's nail is made up of the nail and the quick. The quick is the pink part inside the nail. If your dogs has light-colored nails, the quick may be visible making it easier to avoid. If the nails are black you will not be able to see the quick and will need to be extra cautious not to trim too far back. If you do hit the quick, this is called quicking and is a very painful experience for your dog. It will bleed a lot so immediately apply styptic powder.

Cleaning the Ears and Eyes

The inside of your Malamute's ears should be pink and free from debris. Check once a week and wipe clean with ear wipes from your local pet store. Never use cotton swabs or try to clean out the inner ear as this can cause damage to your dog's ear. If you see anything unusual in your dog's ear, seek a veterinarian's advice quickly before the problem becomes worse.

Your Malamute's eyes should be clear and free from debris. Clean the corners of the eyes daily with eye wipes from your local pet store.

Common Diseases and Health Conditions

Alaskan Malamutes are a generally healthy breed, but they are predisposed genetically to a few health conditions.

Hip Dysplasia–Usually not diagnosed until two years of age, hip dysplasia is not a life threatening disease but instead is one that can greatly reduce the quality of a dog's life. Sometimes hip dysplasia can be managed with drugs, weight control, and monitored exercise. A Malamute with severe hip dysplasia may need surgery to attempt to repair or replace the hip altogether.

Chondrodysplasia–Alaskan Malamutes are genetically prone to chondrodysplasia, a type of dwarfism. This can vary in severity but typically does not affect a dog more than physically being shorter.

Polyneuropathy–This is a debilitating condition that causes chronic weakness and lack of coordination. There is no screening process for this condition and it can affect any Malamute.

Hypothyroidism – Malamutes are susceptible to hypothyroidism. When left untreated, this disease can cause a host of other issues including epilepsy and skin disorders.

Talk to your vet and devise a plan to protect against these genetic conditions. Catching a disease early is the best way to keep your dog happy and healthy for the remainder of his life. If you suspect your Malamute may be suffering from any condition, seek veterinary care immediately.

Holistic Alternatives and Supplements

If your pet has developed a hereditary condition, or if you want to take every precaution to prevent or delay one, the first step toward health and wellness for your Malamute should be a healthy diet. Dogs should have a high protein diet limiting wheat, corn, or soy. Consider skipping the kibble and making your dog a homemade, nutrition-packed meal.

Acupuncture is becoming more common in pets because of its notable benefits in managing pain and increasing circulation. Supporting overall wellness, acupuncture can aid in the treatment of hip dysplasia, allergies, gastrointestinal problems, and pain due to cancer treatments. Acupuncture causes no pain for a dog and is shown to have a calming effect. Acupuncture should only be performed by a certified acupuncturist and you should always consult your veterinarian before beginning any alternative treatments.

Herbs

Herbs are a staple in holistic healthcare but not all herbs are safe for dogs and some can interact with drugs your dog may be taking. Discuss any herbs with your vet before adding them to your dog's diet or lifestyle. Some herbs include:

Goldenseal – Anti-inflammatory and anti-bacterial, goldenseal can be used externally on bodily infections or as an eye wash for infections or conjunctivitis. It can be taken internally at the first sign of kennel cough or digestive issues and can also be beneficial in the treatment of tapeworms and Giardia. Goldenseal should not be used for too long as it can cause stress on the liver.

Milk Thistle – Milk thistle provides liver support by protecting against damage. If your dog is on any medication that can damage his liver, discuss adding milk thistle to his regimen with your vet.

Ginger – Just as with people, ginger is an effective tool for treating nausea and even cardiovascular conditions in dogs. Ginger has cardiotonic effects and can promote functionality of the heart.

Chamomile – Another herb that helps aid digestion, relieve muscle spasms, and reduce inflammation. Chamomile is a great option for treating chronic bowel and gas disorders and can also ease any anxiety your dog may have.

Licorice – Licorice root is a fast-acting anti-inflammatory that can be used for the treatment of arthritis and other inflammatory diseases. It has been shown to enhance the efficacy of other herbs, so it is often combined with others as a part of a treatment plan.

CBD Oil – As stated on the American Kennel Club website, "Currently, there has been no formal study on how CBD affects dogs. What scientists do know is that cannabinoids interact with the endocannabinoid receptors located in the central and peripheral nervous systems, which help maintain balance in the body and keep it in a normal healthy state."

CBD oil, also known as cannabidiol, is thought to treat pain and help control seizures in dogs. Anecdotal evidence also shows that CBD oil may have anti-inflammatory, anti-cancer, anti-anxiety, and cardiac benefits. Discuss with your vet the option of adding a CBD supplement to your Malamute's lifestyle.

These are only a few of the herbs available for homeopathic use for your dog. If you want your dog to experience the benefits of herbal remedies but can't source the herbs yourself, there are many premade solutions and tinctures available for the holistic care of your Malamute. They come conveniently packaged and mixed with directions so you can know you are using the herb correctly. Be sure to only use products from a reputable source that has a reputation for supplying the best holistic and herbal treatments. Beware of cheaper products that may contain synthetics.

Pet Insurance

Although Alaskan Malamutes are generally healthy dogs, they are prone to a few genetic conditions so you may be interested in investing in pet insurance. It is advisable to carefully research each provider to weigh cost versus benefit before taking out a policy. Different companies offer different coverage so be sure to read the fine print and understand any exclusions. Talk with your vet to see if he has a company he recommends.

HELPFUL TIP
Pet Insurance

Pet insurance can help cover the costs of unexpected injuries or illnesses. However, it excludes preexisting conditions and usually requires a waiting period before coverage starts, so the time to get pet insurance is before you need to use it.

Rates will vary based on your dog's age, history, and condition. While it is generally considered more affordable to pay out of pocket for vet visits for common ailments, pet insurance can be a life-saver if something catastrophic arises and your Malamute needs expensive tests, surgery, or medication for life.

CHAPTER 14
Caring for Your Senior Dog

Caring for an aging Malamute can present a whole new set of challenges. Aging dogs, just like humans, typically require more medical care because they are prone to ailments such as arthritis, cognitive dysfunction, cataracts, hearing loss, incontinence, and inability to regulate body temperature.

Not all dogs reach this stage at the same time and many can live comfortable and happy lives for years, even with these ailments. This chapter will discuss potential issues you may face with your aging Malamute and help you navigate the difficult end-of-life decisions when the time comes.

Photo Courtesy of Karen Aldridge

Common Old-Age Ailments

Arthritis – Osteoarthritis is a degenerative joint disease where the bones of a joint rub against each other due to the deterioration of the cartilage between them. This deterioration can cause severe pain, stiffness, and limited mobility. Osteoarthritis cannot be cured but can be treated with medication and supplements to slow the progression of the disease and treat symptoms.

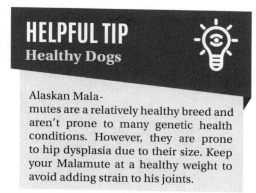

HELPFUL TIP
Healthy Dogs

Alaskan Malamutes are a relatively healthy breed and aren't prone to many genetic health conditions. However, they are prone to hip dysplasia due to their size. Keep your Malamute at a healthy weight to avoid adding strain to his joints.

Cataracts – Cataracts cause a dog to have blurry vision by creating an opacity in the normally clear lens. If your senior dog develops cataracts, have your vet monitor him closely for worsening symptoms. When left untreated, cataracts can sometimes lead to blindness.

Cognitive Dysfunction – Senior dogs are susceptible to dementia just like humans are. If you notice your dog forgetting something he does often or acting unusually out of his normal routine, discuss options with your vet for helping improve his quality of life. If your Malamute experiences these symptoms, try to ease his frustration and confusion by making everyday tasks simpler for him and keeping the layout of your home the same, rather than moving furniture around and potentially confusing him.

Hearing Loss – Hearing loss is common for old dogs. While many will lose some degree of hearing, they may not go completely deaf. Signs of hearing loss include a sudden lack of obedience, increased startle reaction, and excessive barking.

If your dog experiences hearing loss, you may need to find another form of communication. Teach your dog hand signals at the first sign of hearing loss so that if he loses his hearing completely, you can still communicate commands. It may also be helpful to keep a flashlight handy to signal for his attention.

Basic Senior Dog Care

Photo Courtesy of Alan Dukes

When caring for your senior Malamute, there are certain precautions you should take. Care for a senior dog should be focused on keeping him comfortable and happy. Like older people, senior dogs have trouble regulating their body temperature. Be sure your Malamute stays cool on a hot day.

Special accommodations may need to be made to make life more comfortable for your senior dog. If your dog has arthritis, he may benefit from a specially made bed to help with stiffness. If you have stairs, you may also need to consider keeping all of your dog's things on the lowest level of your home so he doesn't need to climb the stairs.

As a dog ages, energy levels usually decline along with stamina. It's important that you give your aging Malamute regular, gentle exercise to keep him in shape. Obesity can be a problem in older dogs who typically move around less, and it can exacerbate other age-related ailments such as arthritis and heart conditions. If obesity becomes a problem despite regular exercise, discuss options with your veterinarian. He or she may suggest switching to a different food.

Oftentimes, a dog's dental care is neglected throughout life leading to potentially painful issues in old age. If your elderly dog suddenly seems to lose his appetite, check with your vet to see if the problem could be dental. Sometimes a painful tooth or painful gums can be enough to deter a dog from his dinner.

Your senior dog will probably need to see the vet more during his last years than he did previously. The AAHA (American Animal Hospital Association) recommends that you take your senior dog to the vet at least once every six months for a check-up. These regular vet visits can help you catch any conditions early and allow for more prompt treatment, potentially leading to a better quality of life for your Alaskan Malamute.

Illness and Injury Prevention

One of the most important aspects of senior dog care is preventing illness and injury. It's much more challenging for an elderly dog to overcome an illness or injury than it is for a younger dog.

As discussed above, exercise is just as important for a senior dog as it is for a young one. It should look a little different, though. Because a senior dog is more prone to injury, exercise should be done at a less vigorous pace that will have less impact on aging joints. Instead of going for a daily jog, take your aging Malamute for a walk or take him for a swim. Avoid activities that involve jumping or climbing an incline. These activities may risk injury or aggravation of arthritis, causing your dog unnecessary pain.

Continue to engage your senior Malamute in mental exercise as well. This can protect him from age related dementia and cognitive dysfunction. It won't prevent it completely but it may help to slow it down.

To protect your senior dog from illness, be sure to continue his parasite medication for fleas and ticks. Also, make sure he stays up to date on his vaccinations. If an elderly dog does fall ill, he is more likely to suffer complications that may be life threatening. A younger dog may contract the common Bordetella bacterium and suffer no real consequences but for a senior dog, a simple infection can quickly turn into pneumonia which may result in a hospital stay.

Photo Courtesy of
Rebeca Miranda

Supplements and Nutrition

Proper nutrition is more important than ever when a dog reaches his final years. His metabolism is slowing down and his quality of life and severity of geriatric conditions can be greatly influenced by diet. There are many foods and supplements on the market that are specifically formulated for senior dogs. Talk to your vet about if and when you should switch your dog to a senior formula.

Before adding any supplement to your dog's diet, consult your veterinarian. He or she may be able to direct you to a quality brand or alert you to possible side effects or interactions with your dog's current medications.

Below is a list of the most common supplements.

Glucosamine and Chondroitin – Two supplements often paired together to combat osteoarthritis, glucosamine and chondroitin have been found to be therapeutic in the treatment of canine arthritis. These compounds are found naturally in cartilage and are made by the body.

When looking for a glucosamine and chondroitin supplement, look for highly reputable brands that source all of their ingredients from the United States. Imported glucosamine has been found to contain many contaminants including lead, especially when sourced from China. Since the FDA does not regulate supplements, the only way to know if you are getting a quality product is to be vigilant and diligent in your research. Even popular pet store brands that say "made in the U.S.A." can include ingredients sourced from China.

Omega-3 Fatty Acids – Omega-3 fatty acids like DHA and EPA have been shown to be beneficial for a number of reasons that may benefit your senior dog. These fatty acids are beneficial for the brain, potentially improving cognitive function in old age and may even give his immune system a boost. According to the American Kennel Club, "The addition of Omega-3 to the diet may [also] help reduce inflammation and can promote cell membrane health."

Antioxidants – Including an extra source of antioxidants in your senior dog's diet can be beneficial as well. You can do this by purchasing a supplement or by simply allowing your dog to snack on high antioxidant fruits such as berries and apples.

Probiotics – Probiotics help maintain healthy bacteria in the gut, the place where up to 80 percent of a dog's immune defenses reside. This can improve immune function and help your senior dog ward off illness and disease more efficiently.

Photo Courtesy of
Kaylie Smith

When It's Time to Say Goodbye

Undoubtedly, the hardest part of being a pet owner is knowing when it's time to say goodbye. Our dogs devote the best years of their life to us, unconditionally gifting us with love and loyalty no matter the circumstances. When the time comes and you see that your beloved Malamute is experiencing more pain than joy, it may be time to consider the most difficult decision you will face in pet ownership.

Many people believe that it is one of the toughest and greatest responsibilities of animal ownership to know when to humanely relieve an animal from the pain when the end of their life is inevitable. It is never an easy decision and often leads to an array of emotions for the owner including sorrow, guilt, and second thoughts. These are normal and will probably never change no matter how many times you face this decision.

How will you know when the time is right?

No one knows your dog better than you do and no one will be able to make this decision for you. You and your Malamute have a bond that nobody else can understand and that is exactly what makes you the right person to make the final call. If you have a gut feeling that your senior dog has made a sharp decline in health and is hurting more than he is enjoying life, it may be time to say goodbye. A few telltale signs that death is imminent are extreme lethargy, lack of interest in anything, loss of coordination, incontinence, and not eating or drinking.

Only you and your dog will know when this time is. Your dog has trusted you with his life during all the time you spent together and he trusts you with it now. If you believe putting him down humanely will end his suffering, speak to your vet and discuss euthanasia.

Once you have made the decision that the time has come to humanely end your dog's suffering, understand that second thoughts are normal. Don't second guess the decision that is best for your dog just because it's hard for you. Grieving over this decision is natural and normal. Talk to a trusted friend or family member to help you cope during this difficult time.

The Euthanasia Process

Before you take your dog to the vet or have your vet come to your home, call any friends or family members who may want to say goodbye. You will have the option to be present when the vet performs the procedure. Although it may be hard for you to watch your dog die, know that it will bring your dog comfort and peace in his last moments if you are there with him, holding him and comforting him.

During the procedure, your vet will administer a solution, typically phenobarbital, intravenously. The solution is usually thick with a blue, pink, or purple tint. The vet may inject it directly into a vein or into an intravenous catheter. Once the solution is injected, it will quickly travel through your dog's body causing him to lose consciousness within just a few seconds. Your Malamute will feel no pain. Breathing will slow and then stop altogether. Cardiac arrest will occur and cause death within 30 seconds of the injection.

Your vet will check for signs of life and will most likely step out of the room for a few moments to give you time to say a final goodbye. Your vet and his office staff have been through this before and will understand the emotional weight of the situation for you. They should provide you with pri-

Photo Courtesy of Katie Solberg

Photo Courtesy of
Doris Thompson

vacy and be a source of comfort if needed. Be sure to make payments and after death arrangements beforehand so you don't have to deal with it after.

Your dog's body may still move after death so don't be alarmed if you see twitching. He may also release bodily fluids and this is also normal. When you are ready, leave your dog and allow the vet to proceed with his remains. If you have chosen to have your dog cremated, your vet will coordinate with a cremation service and notify you when his ashes are ready. If you are taking your deceased dog home for burial, the vet will place your dog's remains in a container and will typically carry it out to the car for you.

Whichever you choose, once you leave the vet's office you will begin the grieving process, remembering that the love and bond the two of you shared will always be in your memory. The bond between an Alaskan Malamute and his owner is one that is understood by few but wished for by many.

Made in the USA
Monee, IL
09 June 2022

97764472R00090